Catalin Damir

THE ANGELS WILL LISTEN

Translation: Mihaela Buruiană

2013 First Edition

This book was written with two thoughts in mind:

"**You** are **gods**; **you are all** sons of the Most High."
Psalm 82:6
And again:
"Jesus answered them, Is it not written in your law, I said, **You are gods**?" John 10:34

All men die, but not all men die completely.

Dedication:

This book is dedicated to a theologian and
a philosopher, both united in their quest for Truth.

Foreword

"With Love and Pain for Contemporary Man" is the title chosen by the Elder Paisios of Mount Athos for his work dedicated to the man of today, who is haunted by day-to-day concerns and by the cultivation of a selfish, self-indulgent ego... This is how the old man chose to reprimand his spiritual sons in an attempt to reveal to them the true reality of Christ who was crucified for our sins. Along the same lines, the author Catalin Damir shares with the man of today the fruit of his deepest search and reflections on *"the wealth of life on Earth"* and, more particularly, on *"the wealth of life after the life on Earth"*, a profound meditation on the final purpose of our lives.

"The beauty of the human spirit lies not in what man could do, but in what he does at a given time in his life", says the author, urging the contemporary man to take action, to bring beauty around him, to have the laborious faith preached by the Apostle: *"faith without works is dead"* (James 2, 14-26).

The three parts of the book are meant to be three steps of spiritual rise to the understanding of the divine plan of creation and development of the human being. Starting from the ideological mistakes made by people throughout history and from the attempt to find the middle way of the correct relationship between man and God, the author tries to answer the greatest hunger of contemporary man: *the hunger for love and meaning* (Father Nicolae Steinhardt).

The sometimes brutal images may shock, but the shock is creative and generates new meanings of man's existence on Earth:

"The Hero, the Saint, the Martyr and Their Failed Version, the Genius" is the shattering title of one of the book chapters, which is a meditation on the rational and affective capabilities of the human being, in the absence of the divine moral component, of the connection with the Creator. *"It is the moral component that gives eternal value and, as such, the only real value, to all human actions"* deeply reflects the author.

"God made the light first. Afterwards, he made the luminaries, as well... but they only give out radiation, which has a material purpose. Light comes from elsewhere", says the author: it is the light of the Holy Spirit flowing from the saints' bodies upon their

passage from the life on Earth to the life beyond (St. Seraphim of Sarov, Abba Sisoes the Great, etc.).

"When you give, at first you give from what you have, then there comes a time when you start giving from what you are", said Father Arsenie Boca. The author is giving himself through this book, in an attempt to help the man of our days to reach "the highest virtue of sanctity", as Father Galeriu Constantin called it, namely rising from one's own sins.

"Nobody is redeemed against their will", relentlessly said the same Father Galeriu, but wishing for redemption is so hard in today's world, in a society of riches, of the never-ending present and of a selfish and self-indulgent ego…

Pr. Paul Cătălin Stoleru

"Ascension of the Lord" Romanian Orthodox Church
Montreal, Canada

Author's preface

To this day, since the Fall of Man, he has been looking for the Water of Life.

*"For an angel went down at a certain season into the pool, and troubled the water: **whosoever then first** after the troubling of the water **stepped in was made whole of whatsoever disease he had.**"* John 5, 4

Like the sick who, in order to miraculously heal, sat at the Bethesda pool and needed someone to help them go first into the pool water, right after the water had been troubled by the angel's touch, so does this book try to push the man into water, with the hope that he will benefit from the angel's touch.

Sometimes, in life, miracles happen, as it did with the paralytic near Bethesda, who sat helplessly by the pool with no one to push him. This sick man didn't know he was being watched by ... Someone. Jesus knowing that the man had been in this poor state for 38 years, wanted to change his life through a miracle. And on a Holy Saturday, He did.

Such wonderful happenings are rare today and the people who are waiting for Jesus… or even those who are not, need the wisdom of the Living Water and, so, a push in the "Bethesda water".

Let us then be heedful, for the angels are listening to our heart and, if they deem it in search for the Truth, they'll come down to touch the water for us … sooner.

Table of Contents:

Part I:
"Who can understand his errors?"

1. The Wisdom of the World and the Wisdom of God . . . . p. 15
2. About Philosophy Outside Religion . . . . . p. 20
3. The Problem of Modern Secularism . . . . . . p. 28
4. The Truth and Man's Power of Understanding . . . . p. 38
5. Power and Knowledge . . . . p. 47
6. Building the Virtues . . . . p. 58
7. On Equity and Justice . . . . p. 65
8. The Religious Feeling or Ecstasy . . . . p. 71
9. About the True Education or the Correct Activity of Man's Life . . . . p. 76
10. A Question about Bach's Music . . . . p. 83
11. The Two Paths of the Search for Perfection . . . . p. 90
12. The End of Catechization . . . . p. 100
13. What is Man? And Why? . . . . p. 104

Part II:
"Let There Be Light!"

14. Questions regarding the Genesis .... p. 113

Part III:
"The Beginning of Wisdom"

15. Fear of the Lord and His Mercy .... p. 181

16. On the Immortality of Man .... p. 183

17. The Hero, the Saint, the Martyr and
    Their Failed Version, the Genius .... p. 185

18. Confrontation between Two Human
    Ideals: the Saint and the Genius .... p. 195

19. Asceticism and Fulfillment .... p. 204

20. Looking through the Eyes of
    the Dark Angel .... p. 214

21. "Vanitas Vanitatum!" .... p. 233

22. The Fight between Cain's Sons
    and Abel's Sons .... p. 239

23. Death, God's Mercy towards Man .... p. 254

24. The Road to the Ladder of Infinite Glory . p. 270

Post Scriptum :

Points of Perspective .... p. 278

∽ PART I ∼

"Who can understand his errors?"

Psalms 19,12

The Wisdom of the World and the Wisdom of God

Many "wise" reflections have emerged over the centuries from the minds and lips of people of all the races and religions, from all the corners of the Earth. Ancient and new civilizations, powerful kingdoms or small tribes, they all had wise men who taught them or advised them, who scrutinized events or attitudes. These wise men had their heart in the right place, an open and quick mind and loved their fellow human beings and the beautiful things this world had to offer.

Yet, whether we talk about the Sibyls or the chiefs of the native American tribes, the ancient philosophers or the modern philosophers, the wise men and leaders of all the religions and kingdoms or empires known throughout history, nothing can compare to the authority of the words uttered by the Holy Spirit, through prophets or saints, apostles or martyrs, or, most importantly, to the authority of the Son of God,

Jesus, who created everything and through whom everything came into being.

The speech of the wise men of the world shows an obvious search for the Truth and answers received from some diaphanous place. To the person who listens to those words and reflections, this sends a message of frailty of the relation with the Truth, the fact that the Truth is only touched by the fingertips, that is, it is not controlled in its entirety. What lacks is the firm authority of its Originator, the feeling of ownership over the Truth. When the wise men bestow the Truth upon other people, they do so from the very little they gathered and they are afraid of upholding their ideas as absolute for fear of error. Error is what defines man's relation to the Truth.

Man does not hold the whole Truth, he only has what was given to him from above and, in almost all cases, he was not given very much. Man only knows a small part of the Truth, intuits another part of it and gropes in the dark for the largest part of the Truth. The wise men know more and intuit more than their less endowed or interested fellow human beings, but they share the same feeling of having borrowed the Truth and especially, the same fear of being wrong in any word they utter or any new idea that has not been verified in practice.

What a great difference we feel when we hear the words of the Holy Spirit, through prophets or saints! Whether what we hear pleases us or not, whether it shocks us because we do not understand it or it frightens us through the power of its message and of its consequences, we, humans, see how the Truth pours out of His words with the tumult of a river and not even for a second do we feel the shyness specific to the wise men. The man declared by the Sibyl at Delhi to be the wisest of men (Socrates) said about himself that **he did not know anything** and that his wisdom was that he did not even assume he knew anything in absolute, while the other wise men around him assumed they knew at least something, however insignificant, but nevertheless, **they knew**.

Socrates is an example of a man with a watchful and alive spirit, who accepts his not knowing the Truth and starts looking for it in the only place with safe chances of finding it: the world of the gods. Consequently, he ends up asking his God about the Truth and ponders about it in his Apology, transcribed by Plato:

"... but the truth is, O men of Athens, that God only is wise; and in this oracle he means to say that the wisdom of men is little or nothing." PLATO "Apology of Socrates"

The fact that God is only one is recognized by almost all religions of the world, and even those that assume several gods speak of a hierarchy that includes an omniscient God. Once this God is found, man asks him the existential questions and, in the words of this God, Truth flows like clear water, without any flaw or error specific to man's limit of knowledge.

Jesus said that He himself was God and that He was the Truth and that everything He said was true and above all, being God, He implied that he had all the answers to all the questions, as everything had been done through Him. So from that moment on, when man made contact with Jesus, man's search had to find absolute answers to all his problems and queries, whether practical (pragmatic-somatic, food and the like), political (governance of all the people), religious (mending of his mortally wounded soul), or theological (knowing and communing with God).

The wise men decided to talk to the people in order to bring understanding and comfort when the people suffered from illness, dictatorship, oppression, injustice, existential questions. But the people did not find complete comfort until they spoke to the Creator himself, and the Creator gave them wise words, soothing in any circumstance, gave them peace of heart. To seal this peace, He spoke with the full authority and integrity of God, Originator of the whole Truth, promising with the soft voice of a parent:

"And surely I am with you always, to the very end of the age." Matthew 28, 20

About Philosophy outside Religion

The entire philosophic phenomenon is a closed road, as more recently modern philosopher Ludwig Wittgenstein correctly found out with the help of his powerful logic.

Philosophy is trying to put a different order in a world already ordered and explained by the Creator. Philosophizing, explaining, putting in order, bringing to a common denominator (to order) all the objects, whether material (microcosm and macrocosm), or immaterial (abstract ideas, concepts, spirit), which are already put in order by the Creator, but without giving the Creator what belongs to Him and even trying to remove the Creator from the equation, in the extremes of philosophy, result in a laughable vision. It is a vision which the "philosophizing" man deems a valuable thing and shares it with everybody as Truth, as something heard from some authority, or from the philosopher, or from a group of philosophers who, somehow, by force of their numbers, gave quality to an idea of doubtful quality. The modern philosophers behave like a choir of "fools for pride" who use complex and pretentious language and, if this "magic" veil is not enough to induce complexes and to overstrain the resistance of the logical, free-minded man, then the choir of fools will start talking "in languages", either snobbishly valuating some foreign words or inventing some "new" term that supposedly means something which cannot be explained through simple words.

All this hand of marked cards is used by the modern philosophers who, by this dying attempt, are trying to save the life of Philosophy as science, forgetting that Philosophy died when Socrates, the spiritual mentor of Plato and by extension, of the classical-ancient and modern Philosophy wrapped together, started looking for a GOD that would explain the world to him. Socrates understood better than anyone that what he called Philosophy was merely **a religious question with a religious answer** coming from the Creator, the sole authority permitted to speak on Creation and so, to speak about the meaning of Man's creation, the reason of his existence. Therefore, Socrates did not build any philosophical system, as he did not think that man could understand Creation by himself, so a human made system will have no value what so ever; and still will not have any value today.

Feeling its ideological death, modern philosophy, like any other "heresy" or stray from the Truth, is trying to approach Religion either by endeavouring to "become useful" in the matter of religious dogma, or by creating a sort of hypnotic hybrid – the "philosophical religion". These two end-roads of philosophy show once again that this fruit, Philosophy, after the coming of Jesus Christ, who opened the Way in asking God directly, will have nothing but a harmful future in this great lesson which humanity calls Life. This happens because Philosophy asks only about the Human Intellect and, so, it cannot receive infallible answers, as is the case with Christian Religion, which gets this kind of answers from the Son of God, through the Holy Spirit, as promised by Him:

*"But the Helper, the Holy Spirit, whom the Father will send in My name, **He will teach you all things** ... "John 14, 26*

Another counter-argument to practicing philosophy is the fact that life, short and eventful as it is, does not hold the time and luxury for man to mull over false ideologies, distorted realities and crazy, meaningless ideas or ideas without a final and spiritually pragmatic conclusion. Life requires focus and a maximum discipline in ideas, so that the child may grow up and become a man in all his plenitude, as envisaged by the Creator, and as such, start on the great and endless road to knowing the Creator, a ROAD that is the only reason of creating Man and keeping him alive in his Creation in the first place.

Many will come and say that the exercise of philosophy can have a positive impact on the mind and that a mind put to work will react with greater ease to any deviation of ideas that the "Evil One" could throw at man. But there are many examples that, when put into practice, show quite the opposite. Man needs simplicity to be able to receive the divine message, which is addressed through the mind to the heart, and not to the mind exclusively. Sometimes the mind can go against the heart in a harmful way.

Being merely an instrument, the mind must be used as simple and clean as possible in translating this message to the heart and not interfere, by pride, between the message and the heart, by altering, truncating or, worse, changing the meaning of the message by 180 degrees. The mind should be controlled rather than put to work and if a man wishes to put his mind to work in order to fight much stronger minds, then this work should be done in a state of complete wakefulness (open heart), to avoid having his mind kidnapped by the passion of pride and starting dictating his own universal order, getting more and more intoxicated with the wine of its false authority. It is the mind that needs to be subjected to the Truth, and not the Truth subjected to the mind.

Pilate asked Jesus: "*What is truth?*". Jesus knew what (who) it was and answered him even before being asked:

"*To this end was I born, and for this cause came I into the world, that I should bear witness unto the truth. Every one that is of the truth heareth my voice.*" John 18, 37

He did not say: use your mind to inquire for the Truth and build from little pieces a mosaic which you can call Truth. Jesus directed man's steps to the Truth because He showed that the Truth was somewhere (in something, in someone) and just needed to be received, being accessible at any time, to anyone, however unsophisticated.

Jesus is the GOD whom Socrates was looking for and who came to answer his question. Socrates, who all his life was a fanatic in his search for the Truth, would have most certainly asked Jesus all the questions he could think of, and Jesus would have most certainly answered either through words or through facts, like in that episode in the Gospel of John with the Greeks who had come to talk to Jesus, and to whom He showed, through the thunder-like voice of His Father, descended from the skies, that He, Jesus, was the son of GOD and a GOD himself and, so, He had the power and authority to talk to them about all that belonged to Him, about the Reality of this world, this experiment called Life and Man - *see the Gospel of John,* Chapter 12, verses 20-32.

The Romanian thinker Petre Tutea dramatically said about his experience with Philosophy:

"I'm trying this experience: I'm trying to disinfect myself from philosophy, from the lice of metaphysics... A friend of mine says: you disinfect yourself from it, but you use its instruments. Yes, but if I get on a train, this doesn't mean that the railway is my god ... In philosophy, one can wander until one gets crazy. The philosophers, what have they accomplished with their autonomy? Nothing! They hold no truth."

A Personal Diary with Petre Țuțea, 1992

Petre Țuțea, a great connoisseur of modern philosophy, who knew most part of ancient and modern philosophy, along with the numerous terms in all the significant European languages, be they dead or still in use, thought that Philosophy wandered and **held no truth.**

Why did such a great thinker, who knew well that his own opinion was much valued in the philosophic community make such a statement? Because he met the Truth, he met the Word of God, who is a person:
"It has taken me a lifetime to acquire **the certainty** *that, apart from the Bible (the Word of God), there is no other truth."*
Petre Țuțea, like a man awaken from the nightmare of the Mind, also stated the following:
"They say that man was endowed with intellect to know the Truth. In my opinion, man was endowed with intellect not to know, but to receive the Truth."

The thinker was well into his old age when he gave over the control of the mind to the heart. It was only then, after a lifetime, that he really understood where he stood in this world. Up to that point, he had been "up a tree", as he points out himself:
"Without the Bible, the Europeans, even those who won the Nobel Prize, would still sleep in trees."

There is a wonderful world, much larger than that of Philosophy, a real world that opens through the gates of Theology.

Theology starts when Socrates, the free man, the philosopher, the lover of Wisdom meets GOD (Jesus Christ) and starts asking his precious questions. And, one after another, his questions are answered either with miraculous words, or with thunder and opening of the skies.

Then man, as a creature bewildered by the beauty and importance of what he has just heard and been shown by GOD, changes and transforms himself in what GOD had intended for him to be in the first place, and starts leaving behind the doubts, the blindness and the anguish to which Philosophy had unsuccessfully tried to give a satisfactory answer.

Man will then look upon this existential anguish and upon the "answers" provided by Philosophy as low, even amusing things, which he could now break down into a thousand pieces and play on his fingers, like they were a string of cheap beads... afterwards, looking away in the horizon, towards the magnificent future shown with love by GOD, he would throw away these "little beads" forever, buried into his godlike child's past, like foolish things from his youth...

The Problem of Modern Secularism

What does modern secularism bring to the common man? I will start answering this question by making a distinction between the original secularism and the modern one.

Secularism, as ideology and religion of the post-medieval era, began in full industrial swing out of man's wish for freedom of ideas and ideology. Seeing the power of his mind transposed in the reality of his daily life through the machines and products at the beginning of this industrial era, man changes his "philosophy of life" and starts feeling a terrible need for independence in terms of religion, ideas, hence the animosity against the monarchic elite, and even in terms of freedom to move on Earth and not only. He does not find a satisfactory answer to all these needs in any of the feudal religions, ideologies and, especially, laws, and thus man starts a fierce fight against them, striking everything he sees and feels as threatening to this complete, long desired freedom.

In all this euphoria of freedom or of search for freedom, man forgets about the fundamental questions he has had even before antiquity, since the beginnings of history. Man forgets about the questions that he would have given his soul to find answers to, and for which he had already given his soul, either to a religion that answered these questions, or to a philosophical ideology, a set of human rules, more or less subjective, more or less complex, answering a larger number of problems. The importance of existential questions consists in the fact that, once answered in a complete and satisfactory manner, they have the power to give man a mighty Gift: complete and eternal spiritual Freedom. Without answers to these questions, man embarks on the road of modern materialist slavery.

The original secularism answered the existential questions through the new religion-ideology called "Science", a rudimentary form of human logic – rudimentary because Science applies sequential, not parallel Logic bounded by Intuition, thus decreasing its complexity to an almost rational monophony (simple though, for example, 1+1=2) at its worst and maybe a homophony at its best (same thought permeating different fields of science). But Science can't reach the complexity of polyphony, which is many thoughts, sometimes moving paradoxically one against the other, but all forming a perfect Song, explaining the Reality as much as we can understand at one point in time, and as such Science is becoming a simple ideological tool to sell to the masses and, so, to manipulate them.

Science answers some of the existential questions based on "empirical, factual evidence", subjectively interpreted to serve the new ideology. The problem is that Science itself brings changes and new interpretations of these "facts" all the time and so, in the end, one remains at a loss and without any certainty as to one's own thoughts or those of another. Man ends up inflicting upon himself a spiritual infirmity, a rational suicide, a suicide through a simple and false logic (sophism). Man loses the practice of Platonic thinking, a logical thinking, but which uses Logic and Reasoning as tools **secondary** to the Intuition of Spirit and, so, follows various logical paths at the same time (i.e. he analyses logically and rationally the multiple roads opened by the Intuition of Spirit), he thinks in parallel at any given time. Because of the uncertainty of his Reasoning, he also loses the power of receiving certain, absolute ideas (points of certainty, principles) from another thinker, religion or ideology. It all becomes a destructive cognitive process which results in the loss of cognition itself, point by point, principle by principle, until all that remains is an unidentified, uncertain being, scared of everything around, especially of the great unknown called Death.

Modern man becomes, through an intellectual self-infirmity imposed by the modern education of Relative Truths (several parallel truths equal no absolute truth), a being that can be easily manipulated by any ideological trend combining any amount of Truth and Lie.

The Romanian philosopher Petre Țuțea made the following remark regarding the Relative Truths:
"*I had the revelation that there is no truth besides God. I think that several truths in relation to God equal no truth. And if Truth is only one, being transcendent in its essence, then it resides neither in science, nor in philosophy, nor in arts.*"

We see here the same conclusion as Socrates, that started his questions by inquiring first the artists, the inventors, the artisans, etc. and seeing that they give unsatisfactory answers regarding the origin and meaning of their main gift.

As long as the industrial era was at its peak and the resources, both human and natural, were abundant, the existential questions and the consequences of the destruction of the natural habitat, human, animal, and botanical were thrown like a hot potato from one hand to another and no coherent and serious answer was provided. Particularly, the existential questions received totally dismissive answers, as if for children, completely unsatisfactory even for those who made them up. But we are slowly getting to the modern part of secularism and these harsh questions are more and more present in the people's minds and hearts.

Modern secularism could no longer promise the "World of the Future", a childlike Utopia where man has evolved, though we don't know how exactly and is so advanced that he has surpassed not only the spiritual human condition (he has almost no vices, only virtues), but even nature itself, by living to an extraordinary age or even attaining immortality and leading an existence ever more "spiritual", yet at the same time an existence without idea, without any clear purpose or end goal to be achieved.

The "World of the Future" answers the existential questions with a sort of heaven on earth in which man lives happily ever after, but in total ignorance as far the existential questions are concerned: who are we?, where are we coming from?, where are we going?, does God exist?, what is the purpose of our existence?, etc.

Modern secularism sees its ideology more and more bankrupted by the conditions of the reality we live in on this planet, conditions which include rampant poverty, uneducated, uncivilized people controlled by vices, natural resources that become scarcer with each passing day for a constantly growing population.

The "World of the Future" dream is gone and, in its place, the existential questions, the wolves of the soul and of the peace of man's mind, show their hideous grin once again. This time, these wolves are more famished than ever and seed despair and helplessness in those who are not ready to answer them, so many unprepared people these days.

Once more, religions take the lead of human aspirations, with more resolution than before, because man has seen for himself what three centuries of industrial material wealth can lead to, both on a personal level and as far as the environment is concerned.

In this modern era, a large number of secularism nostalgics still prostrate, more and more hysterically to their secularist "god", to the bankrupting ideas appeared over the past two – three hundred years, ideas that do not entirely satisfied them. These are ideas with no beginning and no ending, unfinished in the middle.

These zealous prostrators are atheists, ultra-liberal or other kinds of "humanist" who feel these are the last days of their Complete Freedom, gained with so much fight, started centuries ago. They watch with despair the world "falling" once again, from their point of view, into Religion and other mental "prisons", as they see them. These people, prisoners of their own vice, a vice and drug called "complete ideological freedom", forget that people were truly free only when the existential questions were answered in a concise and certain manner, giving them peace of mind and the freedom to enjoy both this and the future life.

The negative effect of secularist atheistic ideologies is that, for lack of other meaningful purpose, they pushed man into a desperate race for improving the material quality of his life or the quality of his status in this world and he no longer has the time to enjoy the simple things life offers to free spirits. Man has ended up not living anymore, but feeling like a beast without a stable shelter, moved from here to there for economic reasons and with a deadline for joy, imposed by the physical death of his body, a deadline that can make any spiritual blind man heartless towards his brothers.

In one sentence, secularism replaced the Eternal Holy Joy with the Hysterical Joy, very limited by time and by the quality of the material life. The joy of God was replaced with the joy given by material wealth, having as secondary effect the development of a spiritual panic that steals into man when his material purpose does not appease his fear or satisfy his hunger of the absolute, when it does not solve the existential equations: truth, death, the futility of ephemeral purposes, etc.

This "modern" joy is hysterical because people do not really rejoice in their material wealth, they merely accumulate it without using it wisely or, worse, they use it to the detriment of their own and their fellow human being's body and spirit. As such, even ephemeral joy becomes hard to obtain in modern times, which are full of poverty and overpopulation and, in the end, man is left only with the despair and helplessness that arise from this pathetic equation: man chases a richness that is getting harder to obtain and, even if he obtained it, he still wouldn't know what to do with it to improve his spiritual situation.

But man's life should not be desperate or pathetic. Life should be harmonious and full of hope. This is possible only if man frees himself from the simplistic equation imposed on man by the sophism (a false answer to a real problem) called atheism and other ideologies based on it. Man needs a steady ideological ground. This wish of looking for the Unique Principle (God), which is the source of all meanings, was as strong for Socrates as it is for each man today. Those who have found this Principle should extract the sap of life from it. Those who haven't found it yet should look for it with the strong belief that they will find it, for God is merciful towards the lover of Truth, towards the ones that search for Him.

Man enters again the Era of the Absolute Principle which gives meaning to Life. How about the secularism nostalgics? Should we wait for their generation to die? Should we wait to see how despair drives them almost insane? Should we wait to see them convert to some ad-hoc religion, created for their personal use, since, out of pride, they will not convert to the Word of the Lord? Whatever history offers us in relation to this subject, it will be a real show to watch for the post-modern man. Depending on the choices of man, on the cultural, philosophical and religious levels, this implosion of post-modernist secularism can be a terrible or a wonderful show for him to watch.

For those who believe in God, this will definitely be a miraculous show, like a second Flood, but watched from afar, from the Ark of faith and of the soul imbued with the Holy Spirit.

While looking with sadness at the people drowned in the waves of despair brought along by the pointless secularist ideologies, we will celebrate having found again the holy eternal life as life's Purpose of the man renewed by his faith in God, the Absolute Principle, the Cornerstone of the entire Creation, the Salvation of the desperate, almost hopeless soul.

Truth and Man's Power of Understanding

Truth cannot be deduced with certainty by the human mind based on the actual facts, based on the Reality presented to man by the sum of his somatic (corporal) and spiritual sensors. Reality is changing constantly and the interpretation of one of its facets will always be contradictory to one or infinite other interpretations of other of its facets.

The interpretation of Reality by man is impossible even when Reality stands still and no change occurs in the laws governing it, laws which are ephemeral according to the will of the Creator (see an example in the Book of Joshua of Navi, Chapter 10, verses 12-14, as well as in other miracles shown in the Holy Bible), because man does not see **the entire** Reality and, even if he saw it, he would not know its final purpose, the meaning of its creation and existence and, as such, the final conclusion of this lesson, the big image.

Even if man had total rational power, he still would not know Reality, as it is fixed only for a certain time or, if we think about it more deeply, Time, as another component of Creation by which the Creator can move freely or which He can remodel as He pleases, cannot stabilize even one facet of Reality enough for man to draw exact and perfect conclusions based on his observation of the respective facet.

In conclusion, Reality is **at the same time** *completely non-uniform and non-stabilized* in one form or another permanently (Time, stopped at its smallest part, still cannot immobilize Reality in a satisfactory manner for man to be able to draw conclusions, as Reality is mobile or modifiable by the Creator outside the temporal and spatial dimension) and yet *completely accessible and UNIQUE* (stable in its supra-form – the totality of all its possible forms), without the possibility of having **more than one interpretation or one Meaning**, for, at any given time, the **totality** of Reality is indivisible and its' meaning is always clear to one Being. Another name of Reality is the Creation.

Creation is thoroughly known by the Creator in any mutation the Creator has decided to make and, so, the interpretation of **the latest version** of Creation is only known by the Creator and nobody else. Thus, the questions must be asked only to the Creator, in order not to risk interpreting Creation the wrong way. For example each child created is another parameter that changes and mutates Creation. Each straw of grass has the same basic power to mutate Creation, as well as each star that is born or dies.

Reality/Creation can only be interpreted through the eyes of **the One** who is constantly creating and recreating it, as He pleases, the miracles of having children (new souls) being proofs of modern divine creation. At the same time that God mutates the Creation, He is in complete control of the final Purpose and Meaning of this Creation, hence His eyes sees Creation's TRUE form and His conclusions about this form are Absolute, so we humans better listen to what He has to say to us, if we want to understand Reality - Creation.

The Book of Joshua of Navi, Chapter 10, 12-14 says: *"Then spoke Joshua to the LORD in the day when the LORD delivered up the Amorites before the children of Israel, and he said in the sight of Israel, Sun, stand thou still upon Gibeon; and thou, Moon, in the valley of Ajalon. And the sun stood still, and the moon stayed, until the people had avenged themselves upon their enemies. Is not this written in the book of Jasher? So the sun stood still in the midst of heaven, and hasted not to go down about a whole day.* ***And there was no day like that before it or after it*** *that the LORD hearkened unto the voice of a man: for the LORD fought for Israel."*

So, a man who is imbued with the Holy Spirit will have access, depending on how much is given to him from above, to seeing Reality through the eyes of the Holy Spirit, hence to its true and unique interpretation. The eyes of the Holy Spirit permanently see the meaning of this Reality, the role of its creation being wholly, completely known to the Holy Spirit, and not just bits and pieces like we see. Thus, **the meaning**, the end purpose or reason of the whole Creation-Reality and the meaning of each small part that constitutes the Creation, of the material it is made of and its inter-relations, is COMPLETELY known by God at ANY given time, or outside time itself, hence ideologically stable/fixed.

We see, therefore, that Reality has only one interpretation in any of its mutations, as all mutations of Reality serve the end-purpose of its initial creation, the declared end-purpose being to evolve the creature with or without her awareness of this fact. Reality-Creation has no finality, its purpose and meaning are dissociated from a given finality because such finality does not exist, it is not a part of the Meaning of Creation-Reality. The evolution of human beings towards the Creator is infinite, because the Creator is infinite in itself.

The opposite of finality, hence the fact of immortality and the act of knowing your Creator, into eternity, is part of this Meaning of its creation.

Socrates, a man whom his disciplined mind could not lie enough as to smother his existential questions, noticed well man's incapacity of knowing the Creation and the answers to the questions related to it. This is why he abdicated from performing any cognitive process connected to the knowledge of Reality and only used questions regarding the structure of Truth, a structure seen as inaccessible to the mind and even to the spirit of man without divine help from the Source. This is the reason why Socrates says he is "a man who knows nothing about nothing" and he looks for a God who would explain to him in detail the Reality-Creation. The Truth, knowing Reality and its meaning, as a final target of man's wishes, can only be **given** to the mind and heart; it cannot be explored by individual or collective human forces, the latter being merely a sum of individual forces, so the quality of exploring would not change even a bit.

The human mind searching for Truth is limited by the fact that it is part of Creation and it does not have the complexity or simplicity of understanding the "material" that Creation is made-manufactured of in its entirety. Creation is manufactured by the Energies of God, which have different forms and textures, whether material or immaterial. Consequently, the human mind does not stand a chance to understand by itself the Meaning of Creation, a **meaning** which is intrinsic to the Material that Creation is made of. Creation is manufactured from its Meaning, because all Energies of God have a clear purpose, a final but infinite Conclusion, which is witnessing and being increasingly in awe of the Glory of God.

Only through the eyes of the Creator of this Material and of the Idea behind this material, which is one and the same as the Material (e.g.: "Let there be light" - *the Idea*; "and there was light" - *the Material*) can one see at any time the Meaning of Creation and its true, fault-free exploration can begin. Truth, which is around and within us, can be felt, experienced, seen with a single set of glasses/eyes – the eyes of the Creator, who chooses to give us this sight depending on the cleanliness of our mind, cleanliness dictated by the purity of our heart, namely by how much we wish to know the Truth and for what end purpose.

The Material, similar to the Meaning of Creation-Reality, is Spiritual, and the materiality of the world we experiment through our somatic sensors is spirit. From the point of view of auto-limited people (i.e. limited by their own will), it could seem that spirit and matter are different, but if we take a closer look, we see that they are one and the same: the Material of Creation in various forms and complexities, all working together according to God's will to guide the Creation in compliance with the Meaning of its creation. The atoms, forms of material energy which, cumulated, can give the shape of a tree or of a stone, forms accepted as purely material, are one of the material forms that this Material can take. The spirit of man, which includes his individuality, is **another** form, this time immaterial. Both forms are spiritual because they are spiritualized energies created by God through His Word.

This is why our body is considered the Temple of the Lord, as the entire Universe is valuable to God, who calls it "very good": Genesis 1, 31:

"And God saw every thing that he had made, and, behold, it was very good."

The entire universe, which our body is a part of, is made by God through God's Word - Jesus Christ. The universe has a dual nature of Idea (creative impulse) and Matter (execution), but to man, during his life, only the state of Matter is visible. After the Parousia, the Second Coming of Christ and the entry into eternal life, man will finally be shown the state of Idea, as said by the Apostle Paul:

"But when that which is perfect is come, then that which is in part shall be done away."

"For now we see through a glass, darkly; but then face to face: now I know in part; but then shall I know even as also I am known."
1 Corinthians 13, 10-12

Between the two forms of Creation, Matter and Spirit, there is a difference of quality of the Material, but both of them are part of the Material of Creation, part of Creation. They both took shape by the exclusively spiritual energies of the Lord.

They are both part of this Reality/Creation completely *non-uniform and non-stabilized*, and at the same time, *totally accessible and UNIQUE (stable) in form*, depending on the eyes through which one looks at it.

Thus, the Science of man will not be able to give complete and, so, true answers to any problem. Science, which is the sum of the human intellectual/mental attempts of knowing parts of the Truth, of the Reality/Creation, and the action of drawing conclusions based on these observations, is limited by the lack of an **infallible** source of interpretation of the phenomena it observes.

Man needs to be taken outside the cave (see the Myth of the Cave - Plato) in order to see with his own eyes what God tells him about. But man cannot leave the cave by himself. He needs a Guide, a Saviour, an Interpreter in order to be able to see and interpret the expression of God's perpetual will, which is the Creation and, so, to know the Truth.

Power and Knowledge

Knowledge means Power.

Power wants Knowledge because it wants even more Power.

Knowledge leads only to the wish of power because Knowledge comes from God, it is imbued with God's power. Is wanting knowledge the same with wanting God? Is it the same with wanting to "be in God", to "live in God"?

Can knowledge lead to the Lord? Knowledge comes from the Lord and, on its way to us, the closer it gets to our level, the more it degrades. Can the road to God be reversed by a more and more pure understanding of the Truth? Can we apply a reverse engineering of knowledge to get into His thoughts or, at least, to better know the Lord? What is knowledge? Is it a vehicle of God's thoughts or at least of God's capacities, functions and abilities? Or it is no such thing and, if not, then what is the purpose of knowledge? By finding the purpose of knowledge, we find what knowledge is.

In order to get to the Lord, what we need is not knowledge, but being saturated with the Holy Spirit, having our soul identify with God's will. Those who want power want knowledge, because they wish for all God's power, down to the last drop. Given the addiction of power and the very purpose of its existence, which is to have absolute control over everything, is it allowed for someone else than God to have complete power? If God is the only one with complete (absolute) power, then all the others who wish power are usurpers deep down inside and damned never to access absolute power, for God will not lose it willingly. Another reason why He will not lose the Power is because **He is this Power.** It is built in his Essence.

It is perfectly logical for someone that has Absolute Power to never lose it again. It is a feature of power itself to protect its complete, undivided nature. Power cannot be taken or divided by force, without the will of its holder. So the problem consists in identifying the one who holds and has always held absolute power in order to see who will never lose it despite all the creatures' attempts to absorb, take, steal, obtain co-ownership of at least some parts of power. Power belongs and has always belonged to a single Being. This Being lends it to whomever and however He pleases, as much as He pleases, and He can also take it back, increase it, diminish it or alter it in any way He chooses.

Power resides in one place only and it can never be taken by anyone from its holder.

And then, what is this wish for power, felt by man or the Devil? What is the "what if I were God" thought that crosses the mind of any creature at a given time? Where does it come from? What did the Devil think when he wanted to usurp, transfer, God's power? Most definitely, the Devil did not lack information or, at least, he wasn't entirely uninformed about the place of power and its eternal stability within one being. Why did he want something he could never have and risk his privileged place in the structure of Creation? We are told that it was because of his wish for power, the wish to take God's place. This wish, as it has been seen in numerous cases, can be greater than the obvious fact that sometimes one does not stand a chance to get what one wants. In case of the Devil's wish, it's more about a wish for complete freedom from the structure created by God. Some of the guilt seems to have lied in the way the Devil interpreted the knowledge he had from God.

Knowledge, like power, is given and attributed by God to each creature in the various ways and degrees in which He sees fit, in the unique and personal manner in which it can be most efficiently received by the creature. It is given with a certain purpose and it is this purpose that defines the way in which knowledge should be received. It seems that the way in which the Devil received knowledge was influenced by his wish for power. With his eyes and especially his heart, looking at the Absolute Power, the Devil took everything God offered him in terms of knowledge in order to use it for the rebellion he felt ready for, at the time, with at least a fake feeling of possible success. Apparently, he did not have enough knowledge to feel that he could not possibly succeed against God or, if he did, then his wish for power made him lie to himself and to others, many others who shared his wish.

It is interesting to note how the two trees in Eden were assigned. One is the Tree of Knowledge, the other one is the Tree of Life. We see how man is not allowed to taste the Tree of Knowledge until he is ready. Man would have definitely been permitted at some point to eat from the Tree of Knowledge, otherwise why would the Lord have put it there? Does God do things without any meaning or without giving them sufficient consideration? The Lord put the tree there to prepare man for a proper relationship with Him, but it seems that the first step (level) of man's relation with God is not and should not be the access to knowledge. This is why it was forbidden to eat from this tree. It seems that the first step was obedience. It also seems that man failed right from the beginning of the relationship, which was probably the most important step. Man named the animals and was invested with authority over the entire material creation in the name of the Lord, but he failed and still fails in this authority as long as he does not act in the name of the Lord. If man does not act in the name of the Lord, he loses his authority completely and only in certain cases did God give again some of this authority (and of His power), and only for a short period, in a controlled manner, to persons, some saints, who obeyed His will and to priests to accomplish their task of bestowing the Holy Spirit and the Holy Sacraments upon people.

What would it be like if God's angels stopped doing God's will? What would happen to the creatures they were asked to watch over? Actually, some of the angels refused the authority (God's will) and lost their right to speak and act in God's name. They are now "used" by God without being aware of it or without having been informed of the Divine Plans. They are blind. Super-intelligent and knowledgeable, blind creatures, without a meaning or complete order in their actions. They only have an incomplete order... and this equals having no control whatsoever over anything they do. There is a reflection of them in the modern people who are intelligent, but live in an incomplete order, dissatisfactory on the spiritual level. When one does not know and will never know all the steps of making a watch, how can one manufacture that watch? The Divine Plan is still manifesting itself unabatedly, as the Lord has the absolute power and knowledge, but without these wretched creatures being able to perceive it.

In fact, God's good angels cannot perceive it either without the Lord giving them understanding of all or at least some parts of the Plan, as He pleases. As each creature is part of the great Divine Plan, will such creature be granted access to knowing such Master Plan down to the last detail? God will decide this, as well as whether to take back what He has given.

At some point, man could see the angels and even the divine manifestation, but this knowledge/power/understanding was taken from him. These days, every once in a while, as Gods wishes, man is given some of the old powers with which he was endowed at the beginning of his creation. It all depends on how man's relation with God is defined. Obedience or knowledge? Man wants God, but how, in which way? Does he want Him to access his power? Does he want Him as a trampoline to a function that is an integral and indivisible part of God's essence itself (power)? Or does he want Him to know His will, to live together with his Creator in the Creation brought to light by the Lord, for him?

When God's apprentices asked which of them would be the greatest, a logical question that shows the wish to have a hierarchy and to know it in order to go up that ladder and to use this knowledge in a way influenced by power, they practically asked what they had to do in order to go as far up as possible in the hierarchy they proposed to God, and Jesus (the Lord) proposed or showed them ANOTHER hierarchy: *"...for he that is least among you all, the same shall be great"* Luke 9, 48

Some interpreted this answer of Christ as a reversal (through humility) of the hierarchy proposed by the apostles in their question or even a postponement of this hierarchy based on power or on the wish for power until they enter the kingdom of God. Only the way in which Jesus answered reveals that He did not want a reversal (reversal in the mirror, but the principle stays the same) or a postponement of the power-based hierarchy, but He proposed a dissolution of the concept of hierarchy or a simplification of this hierarchy to perfection: God the Almighty over everyone else, and the others should consider themselves small and insignificant... Practically, Jesus proposed and validated a hierarchical relation formed of only two persons: God, as holder of the Absolute Power, and the creature, as fulfiller of God's will; nothing more in this relation in terms of hierarchy. Anything else comes from the Evil one or is plainly ... evil.

The fact that God reserves the right to make classifications of the level of sanctity, as He did when He said about John the Baptist in Mathew 11, 11: *"Among them that are born of women there hath not risen a greater than John the Baptist notwithstanding he that is least in the kingdom of heaven is greater than he",* is used by Him as a didactic tool over the creatures in His entire Creation. Who made John the Baptist, right from the womb of his mother, the greatest of all those born of women and the smallest in the kingdom of God? God did!

God can work with the levels of power and saint authority He attributes a creature and He can do this dynamically (by taking and giving) depending on His relation with that creature, and on how He uses that creature as a model to educate other creatures.

Man does not need Power, either absolute or partial.

Man needs the One who already has Absolute Power. Man should want the One who handles Absolute Power, but not to access His power, because only by living with and in God, man has nothing to fear, nobody can do anything without power against the Power of God and against the One who has Undivided Power. Power, like God and Knowledge, is indivisible and, so, one does not need it to protect oneself from powerless creatures that try to fight God, as Power only exists in one place. This is why fear should not exist when one lives in God, as says the Psalm:

"Yea, though I walk through the valley of the shadow of death, I will fear no evil: for thou art with me." Psalm 23, 4

If man wishes to access something, he should try to access God's deep feelings ... the love of the Lord. This is **the beginning of the road** that God laid before Adam. But before accessing God's love, man needs to obey the Lord. What a beautiful example God gave us in the obstacles we find in educating our children! We try to show our children our love for them, but they fail their first step, obedience, and so we don't get too soon to teach them our love, but have first to teach them obedience. Thus, this dull relationship deprived of the goodness of love is maintained until our children manage to surpass the level of disobedience. The same happens with us and God.

What is there to do? What is the proper attitude with respect to knowledge and the wish for knowledge? We have to be pure, the pureness of the heart is defined by the honesty of man's relation with God and His Creation, and to strive to become as pure as possible, as we don't know when God will send knowledge on us. When He sends it, we have to be careful, because the way we use such knowledge will turn us into God's friends or enemies.

Knowledge is a test both of our loyalty and of our obedience. God decides how much knowledge and of what level He sends to man at a given time. Man does not have to wish for knowledge, but merely to wait for it and to become wiser for the time he gets it.

Knowledge is neither a purpose in itself, nor a human instrument, but a godly tool which must be used like power... in the name of the Lord and according to God's will. Thus, this test, like the test given to the angels before us, will prove to us what we truly wish to be: creatures who love God or creatures who strive through any means to get to the Lord's throne in order to do our ... devilish will.

Building the Virtues

Virtues, as some of them are presented in the Sermon on the Mount, are the peak to which the fallen Man must climb, the peak from which he fell and where, before being a fallen Man, he used to live naturally and without effort.

The un-fallen Adam, although he did not possess all the virtues in a complete way, had a good start and, more particularly, he did not bear the consequences of his Sin, which would have prevented him from improving his virtues. These days, the consequences of the Sin (disobedience) are so present in man's life that everything that was natural and easy to do doesn't seem so anymore.

The un-fallen Adam had not been in contact with death, pain, violence, injustice, unhappiness, lack of mercy, lie, fear of his fellow human beings, fear of inanimate objects, fear of animals, fear of angels, fear of shame, fear of rejection or of not being loved. We see in the life of small children how these fears are introduced one by one, we see how unnatural they are and we wonder why we are not able to dominate them and overcome them as before the Fall of Man. If we managed to overcome them as easily as we are scared by them, then we would get to virtues sooner and we would not descend into the same sins again. We would learn from these mistakes.

Nevertheless, the truth is that sin and its consequences are constantly within us and even after we make efforts to clean ourselves, we fall again easily and we rise very hard. The simple logic of rising from our sin would be this: since it is neither natural, nor logical to fall into sin, once we can distinguish sin from virtue, we will not sin again. But it is not so for the reason that sin is not a state of mind and it cannot be overcome by some logical, cognitive process. Only through a process of collaboration of our spirit (our inner self) together with energies that are coming from God's Essence could we succeed in this work of repair of the human spirit.

Yet, man cannot collaborate easily with God precisely because of the vicious circle Sin has put him in. Once a sinner, man can no longer collaborate with God on a daily basis on account of his disobedience and he falls even deeper in his sin. Sin generates even more sin and stopping from committing sin is both an art and a science, and it resembles a "recipe for success" with an infinite number of variables, some of which work against the others. In other words, man needs **guidance** to manage to apply this impossible recipe for success.

In the life of our Saviour, man sees what he should think and do and he finds it easy and natural to think and do, but, when it comes to acting, he sees that his sinful heart draws him to sin and he can't trick it with logical arguments or material or even spiritual prizes to thus turn his heart towards building virtues.

The heart is sick, addicted to the drug of sin. A man addicted to drugs understands perfectly that the drug, be it alcohol, cigarettes or powder, enters his body as chemicals and his body reacts to the drug one way or another, forcing it to want nothing else but drugs. From some point on, the drug doesn't even give him pleasure anymore, but the addict takes it in increasing quantities in order to stop his uncontrollable hunger for drugs, like in the legend of the mythic king Erysichthon, who was condemned by the gods to eternal hunger and who, having spent the fortune of his entire kingdom on food and being left with no other resource, ended up eating his own body. Erysichthon did not eat for pleasure, but to appease the pain in his stomach. Similarly, the fallen man tries to appease his pain caused by sin with even more sin.

The next phase in the search for Virtue is the one where man more or less understands what virtue is, either seeing others or experimenting himself, and then he starts on the road to knowledge, to the discovery of Good and Evil. Man seeks to become wiser.

This search becomes painful when we try to attain virtues and fail or succeed only for a little time. Falling again, man feels like another mythic king, Tantalus, who tasted from the gods' nectar and then was punished by them, for another fault, to be forever hungry and thirsty, close to food and water but unable to touch them, however much he tried, and thus, insatiated and always in need, to live the agony of unsatisfied wish. This longing for virtue, the wiser man feels daily is hard to overcome without extraordinary efforts from him.

Certainly, when an extraordinary effort is made to acquire virtue, many times it tends to be selfish, an effort for something personal, to the detriment of the services which man provides for his fellow men and which his family, children, friends or even unknown people – the entire society - depend on. Sometimes, for this effort to be sustained, man uses the services provided by other people in order to dedicate more time and energy to this personal effort. Thus, the effort can have a selfish cause and, more or less because of it, this effort does not succeed in acquiring any virtue, on the contrary, it tends to attract more sins.

There is also an outstanding personal effort wisely guided towards not becoming filled with egoism, but the difficulty here consists in remaining a consistent effort in this world, where it is difficult to survive and to please everybody.

When they are not involved in an athletic program of acquiring virtues, like the monks, common people, who live in this imperfect world and each day take contact with its ephemerality, can build virtue only step by step, thought by thought, deed by deed. The man in the world has more falls than rises, but these rises are all the more important as they are difficult to obtain. However small these personal victories are, they show the character of such a man and the direction towards which he pulls, more often as slowly as a snail.

With total focus and experienced guiding, most people will manage to get to virtues and escape sin, with the all-present help of God. But when a man is prevented by hard conditions to follow the "recipe of success" and yet he manages to get even an embryo of virtue... that says a lot about him.

The embryo of virtue shows that man's availability for deification. God gave the commandment: "be fruitful and multiply" so that man become wiser by contact with other people who either help him or prevent him from following his road to deification, forcing him to overcome more sin in order to acquiring virtues.

Thus, it is the man most tried and poor in virtues who will understand their value and will thank in tears for any bit of wisdom and start of virtue which God helps him taste. With God's huge mercy, he can possess it for eternity without falling out of that virtue ever again, until the end of his life on earth.

God's gifts belong to God, but man's effort is without a doubt completely his own. As Adam's fall did not require an utterly monstrous fault, like murder or destruction, but merely a disobedience in principle, so does the return to God first take place in principle and then, with God's mercy and without any kind of personal pride, man climbs slowly, with small steps, to the numerous virtues offered by God, to the felicity of man on earth and, especially, to the eternal life.

On Equity and Justice

The act which most grieves us is the act of injustice, by which we understand an injustice or trauma we either witness or participate in with our soul and body.

Justice, as the natural state, the state of good, which all the world creatures live in, is part of the natural order of the world, of the Material of Creation. Seeing injustice means seeing with one's own eyes the destruction of a small part of this beautiful (ecstatic) Creation, destruction which is more than a sensible soul can take, considering the act of love which God made when He created the surrounding world for us.

Man was made with love out of Love (God) and he bears the image of love impressed on his face, so that, even when he seems fierce and mean, a perpetual feeling of mercy can be felt within him, mercy which is most of the time ignored. Yet, we can feel it and this is why, with red eyes on the verge of bursting in tears, we ask the destroyer for his mercy. The act of asking for mercy takes place one way or another because, deep down inside, in the soul of the person causing destruction, there is a chance of waking God's face, the face of the mercy within him.

Man does not enjoy destroying, but he is possessed at that time by his own sinful wishes. He causes injustice with half a soul, the possessed half. The other half, the just, good, kind one is taken prisoner during the act itself, but it remains more or less awake and regrets starts even before committing the ruthless and unjust deed.

When the prostitute is brought to Jesus to be judged (John, Chapter 8, verses 2-11), we witness one of the decisive moments of Divine Justice on Earth. It is then that the divine judgment parts with the human one and teaches man, again, both Equity and Justice in their natural form, a form of NON-DESTRUCTION, of love.

Certainly, according to the word of God, given to Moses to regulate the life of the Jews, the prostitute could be condemned to bodily and spiritual destruction, for, by dying in sin, she would have seen the Inferno. These harsh rules were given to the Jewish people so as not to spread the sin in the recently created community, who had left Egypt with lots of bad, pagan habits. Jesus teaches that Moses and his people received rules from God, who were given to them considering the heart of the people he was leading out of Egypt. So the punishments were increased because their sinful heart did not understand spiritual subtleties. They could not even bear to listen to God's voice when He communicated with them from Sinai Mountain (see Exodus 20 verses 18-21).

But the Holy God, the Word full of Love, came to Earth to teach us that He does not want to harm even a hair on man's head, but to redeem him and help him see Heaven for Eternity. The will of God is for us to see Heaven, and the Lord works with all His might for this to happen, without nevertheless violating anyone's free will.

Even before the Flood, God gave a clear order **against the death punishment, including for criminals**, by His two words in the Book of Genesis:

"Then the LORD said to him, "Not so! If anyone kills Cain, vengeance shall be taken on him sevenfold." And the LORD put a mark on Cain, lest any who found him should attack him." Genesis 4, 15

And again:

"If Cain's revenge is sevenfold, then Lamech's is seventy-sevenfold." Genesis 4, 24

Then Jesus, through His powerful word, set free the prostitute both from the hands of tough, ignorant, insensitive and ruthless people and from the hands of Sin and, so, of the devils in Hell.

The prostitute did not even receive the proverbial **slap on the hand**, but merely a question and good advice. But what question?!! A question that tells us how we should approach the entire Creation: "Where are your accusers?"

The accuser is only one and he is neither Man, nor Holly. He is Satan, as it is shown to us in the Book of Job. Us, people, we have to be the image of God on Earth, the Salt of the Earth, the expression of His love for the entire Creation. Weren't we given this earth, with everything on it, to master? We were given mastery over the earth to apply the Equity and Justice of God, mercy, forgiveness and love towards the guilty one, not to enforce the "justice" of the Devil, seeking revenge, hurting and killing the guilty!

The holy martyrs back in the time of Roman persecutions understood God's message of judgment and chose to die rather than fight and destroy their oppressors. Doesn't God have at any time the power to stop any action that should be stopped? He even has the power to act so as to not even get to that. Then how do we explain the fact that God doesn't stop it? Is it just man's free will and God keeping His promise to let man be free? Or is it a trial, a terrible trial, but which bears God's approval, to test man's faith, to purify him like the metal is purified by fire?

In Job, we see that his friends thought correctly from the human and even logical point of view, but we are not asked to judge with the human logic and equity, devilish by its ruthless rightness, but with our heart of saints of God. Job was deemed righteous before the Lord not because he admitted to God in a scared or servile way that He was in the right, but because he understood the great lesson of love that God gave him. Job understood the Lord and God taught Job the "love for his enemies" even before coming to Earth in human form, as Jesus Christ and teaching it to the disciples and the Pharisees, face to face. Loving one's enemies is only a piece of the Great Lesson, as important as the love for flowers or animals.

The lesson goes like this:

Love the Creation and protect it, help Me repair what Man has broken for centuries.

Therefore, man must repair the Creation together with his God: godly brick with human brick, godly mercy with human mercy.

The Religious Feeling or Ecstasy

Man, a sentimental and rational being at the same time, tends to oscillate between these two "perceptions": feeling and reason. He could live in full command of both his faculties, of both his "perceptions", but he, weak and easily corruptible creature, alternates between the two and chooses to live split in two, forever bearing a hidden regret in his heart. This regret comes from his not living his life completely.

For an important part of his life, he looks for something that would make him feel fulfilled, an ideal he could serve. Man also looks for something that could make him feel complete, perhaps some kind of occupation or purpose that would help him focus on becoming a whole man. He wishes with all his being to not be forced to choose between his heart and his mind. Is there a way that does not cause regret? A road that is clear, serene and fair? Is there a road that generates only happiness and fulfilment for himself and the people around him? This road will have to merge his heart and mind and put them in a common, identical state for a shared purpose.

Some find this state of balance in painting, others in music, in poetry or even in fantasy, and some in the scientific research of Creation. But in all of these cases, the state of grace disappears and reappears at intervals that cannot be completely controlled by man's actions. Of all the feelings that join mind and heart, only one manages to solve the problem of the lacking state of grace: the religious feeling.

The religious feeling has been mistaken by many people with various other feelings, some of which completely opposite to this unique state of inner life. The feeling of grace, of godly gift cannot be confused with anything else once it is experienced. Only those who experienced the state of humility sweetened with hope and indescribable happiness, with beauty and love for everything, can relate to someone who has experienced the same state. It is a state that causes tears not out of sadness or even happiness, but because the spirit, being joined with the mind and the heart, lives fully with the Creation and the Creator and crosses the boundary of matter and spirit, understanding and receiving God's hidden secrets.

The spirit feels and sees that living in this state is a personal choice, and that the Creator doesn't prevent him from reaching Him or from staying in this **complete state** of life. And then the spirit experiences the fear of happiness, the fear of changing his life, the fear of feeling the fullness of heart and mind, of seeing the Reality, the Truth. Yes, this fear exists and is real. It expresses itself by the withholding or even blocking of the tears that come down naturally on the cheeks of the ecstatic. The ecstatic finishes brutally his meeting with the Creator, making a promise to Him and to himself in the most solemn and honest manner that he will come back to this inner place of his heart when he is more ready to face the Creator again. Later on, he realizes he has to postpone the meeting with the Creator as he goes back to making wrong and sinful choices in his everyday life and does not take enough time to double back. Thus, he no longer feels able to bear the vicinity of God in their common place, in his heart.

The state of grace is the natural state man should live in all his life and it is kept by the choice man makes. In his daily life, man is put before several equations that force his choice and have a single correct answer. Man knows the correct answer, he can educate himself to recognise it in his heart and discipline himself to listen to it, thus bringing the state of daily and perpetual grace upon him.

The saints lived in a continuous state of grace as they always made the right choice. The saints' heart and mind did not regret any of their correct choices. Regret only appears when the choice is obviously wrong and hurts someone: oneself, the Creator or the others. Thus, the religious feeling brings peace and happiness to the heart and mind of man, joining them in this life and then completely, in the afterlife, which is eternal.

Being in this state of grace, man begins to receive one by one many sensible "gifts" from the Creator, like some sort of rewards which are, in fact, steps required for man's inner evolution. These presents, spiritual gifts, were given to many saints or "improved" men and they cherished them deeply, with all their heart, and they also pleased and helped others with them. This is why pilgrimages are made to the places where these saints or men of God lead their life which, from afar, seems an insignificant routine in the history of mankind, but when taking a closer look, it appears as a godly life, a life of a godly child on earth. This is the reason why the lives of the saints have such a powerful and obvious impact on other people's lives. One can see in them that the religious feeling is lived in a disciplined and conscious way, wanted so much by the common man.

When man, saturated by the sin in his life and the war between the heart and the mind, consciously and unabatedly starts looking for the religious feeling, the first gift through which all the other gifts come – faith – begins to imperceptibly settle in.

Real faith, which, among others, means the wish to know God, is the beginning of the graceful life, and living it induces the permanent state of grace. The gift of true faith is absolutely necessary for the Creator to bestow upon man the other gifts, as well, so that man perceives and understands them in their unaltered form.

Man should not look for ecstasy as a purpose in itself. What he should do is live in ecstasy as a prior condition for following his spiritual, pastoral road to the Creator, free of error. This is the meaning of the Savior's promise that man would see God's Kingdom on earth **while still alive**.

About the True Education Or the Correct Activity of Man's Life

Modern man lives in a world where education is focused on increasing the capacity of production. All the subject matters that young people learn in school directly or indirectly create men concerned with the material life, in general, and with the production of wealth, in particular. The interesting thing is that modern society, as it is organised today, does not permit man to get rich from only his salary, so that the young man would have the necessary time and resources to make himself a family, to take care of it and at the same time, improve his soul. So, creating wealth-producing persons involves forcing the young person to develop from school the wish to work, while being spiritually confused about the **final purpose** of this lifetime effort.

Eventually, we must ask ourselves **why** does man have to waste all his life producing wealth he can't enjoy while he's young and sometimes he cannot enjoy it even when he's old?

This activity seems to have as purpose a mental/somatic labor, but not in order to create the spiritual conditions necessary for man to develop his relation with the Creator or to investigate himself in view of his spiritual development, as was the initial plan when he was banished from the Garden of Eden, so he can retrace his steps and learn from his mistakes. This modern mental/somatic labor rather seems the result of an ideology that breeds slaves and does anything in its power to keep them mentally busy so they wouldn't think of the conditions in which they are forced to live or see the obvious absurdity of this situation.

Thus, the modern schooling is designed not to educate, but to deepen man in his spiritual ignorance, stealing the educational meaning from the educational act itself. This modern education only manufactures spirits that are dead and unprepared, easy to manipulate and bodies suited to be exploited.

It is for this reason that many educational subject matters dating back to Antiquity have lost their initial purpose and were treacherously converted into the opposite of what they were originally meant to be. One of these subject matters is Philosophy, the love of wisdom.

Philosophy started to materialise in a subject matter of study back in the Greek Antiquity. Its most simple definition would be "asking existential questions more (directly) or less (indirectly), in order to eventually find out the purpose of man's life on earth". The ancient Greeks understood that Reason, being one of gods' gifts, had the capacity of revealing gods' plans to them only if they paid enough attention to the surrounding world which they used as a divine guide or book to seize the meanings of the creation of the world and of man. Therefore, the ancient disciplined their reason enough to not make deduction mistakes and to search the world for a spiritual purpose. The Greek philosophy had a final theological purpose.

Consequently, Philosophy, along with some of the related subject matters, such as Logics, Ethics, Aesthetics, Oratory, etc., was used to educate the spirit for self-knowledge, as well as for knowledge of the surrounding world. Out of Philosophy, later on emerged the subject matters that deal concretely (directly) with the rational knowledge of the world, such as: Mathematics, Physics and, in the subsequent eras, Chemistry, Biology, etc. These new subject matters were meant to help answering the major questions of Philosophy, by providing Philosophy with as many data as possible about the surrounding world. Philosophy interpreted these data through different methods and used them to create the philosophical systems that explain the world, life, man's purpose on earth, etc. We can definitely conclude that the goal of Philosophy **was not** to gather wealth on earth.

Thus, we can easily identify the difference between the purpose of the ancient Greek school and that of the modern school. The ancient school educated and developed man's spirit by creating educational tools that would help him in his **inner** search. The modern school confines man in technical and production fields, one more limited in purpose than the other, depriving him of the freedom and time to analyse himself, and denying him the development of his personality and even originality by forcefully feeding the young man with "scientific" ideas interpreted according to a certain ideology targeting to turn men into slaves, and by guiding him to an **outer** search which is eventually futile.

The young man no longer has the time and frame of mind to analyse himself and is forced by the "realities" of the society he lives in to set himself a purpose of material production or, in many cases, of material survival, instead of finding spiritual ideas that would set him free from this finite universe.

The Antiquity produced spiritually free men who, even as slaves, were free in mind and spirit, for example, Epictetus and his philosophy. The modern era produces men enslaved by the materialist and immoral ideology (e.g. the destruction of the planet's biosphere or abortion), men who, even when they think they are spiritual, are nothing more than creatures guided towards a material road. Certainly, there are and always will be numerous exceptions, but as a general rule, the modern school will turn man into a craftsman, an artisan, not into an intellectual free from the constraints of the material ideology. It is a school of slaves for slaves. Even the so-called modern intellectuals, produced on the line in the ultra-expensive universities of modern society, are put to work for the elite that only think of wealth and power on earth. This way, they become activists without any spiritual value, as their agenda is tainted by an inferior mindset pushed on them by the powerful elites.

Work was held in great esteem in Antiquity, as a noble occupation, but not the noblest. The noblest occupation was Philosophy, the love of wisdom, as what could be nobler than becoming a wise man, close to the gods? These days, the purpose of school is no longer to guide men to wisdom but only to craftsmanship, which would benefit the oligarchic elite that runs the world with an iron hand, through a criminal and brutish ideology, so far from the spiritual side of man.

Nothing is without purpose and we should ask ourselves why the purpose of school has changed fundamentally, and the young men who have access to wisdom through the subject matters taught in school are directed exclusively ideologically, whatever the political system under which they live, to a ***craftsmanship ideology***.

The answer consists in the fact that those who look for wisdom cannot be easily subjected and manipulated, while those who are subjugated by the wealth and benefits of the modern material life are terribly easy to manipulate. And if someone does not allow himself to be subjugated by these material benefits, then the system impoverishes him sufficiently to make him think only of survival.

In the end, the subject matters are the same in the modern school, but the school curriculum and the teachers' requirements are critical for a correct understanding of such teachings and for setting the young men's purpose in life. It is rare these days that we get to see young people dealing with True Education, most of them only deal with "education".

Of course, teachers have the ability to guide such young minds towards True Education, but… will they do it? Will they go against their human masters? That will be called heroism.

A Question about Bach's Music

Did Bach realize what impact the complexity of his music had on his listeners? What pleasure is there in listening to cultural music? How does one get to understand cultural music, even through a Spartan learning discipline? Is this music made only for those who are initiated in this art, as professionals? Or it has nothing to do with that, but with the gift of understanding that each of us possesses?

Cultural music, sometimes known as classical music contains in its very name the reason why some people don't understand it or don't participate with all their heart in the joy it gives: one must be a cultivated man, meaning knowledgeable, both complex and simple in thought, profound, with distributive attention and, at the same time, able to stay focused on the "whole picture".

According to the history of music, cultural music, which was originally a spiritual and religious occupation, started to become more and more complex in expression, thus trying to force the listener's ascent to the heights reached by the composer and even farther. It is at the same time a vehicle and a channel. Some would say it is a mere tool which the soul can use to discover and then use the energies hidden within, towards a concrete purpose known only by our inner self.

Bach knew the rule above and wrote music for people who wish to evolve, who dive wholeheartedly into this search for perfection, using music, among others. It is with this conclusion in his heart and mind that Bach wrote his music. This composer, although prolific, was not interested in the trivial and vulgar (inferior) way in which the masses use music as a sonorous decorative object, a material object, after all, which tickles one's senses in a somatic way, along with food and carnal pleasures.

J. S. Bach was interested in the "breeze" of the Holy Spirit.

This is why we feel in Bach's music the melancholy and mourning for the Lost Paradise. In the music of this inspired composer we feel a beginning of perfection that delights us more than anything in this world, precisely because it does not refer to something in this world, at least not the world perceived by the materialistic, narrow-minded and grossly calculated man. There are also other spiritual "tools" that can express even more powerfully the states experienced by soul through music, which we will not enumerate here, but suffice it to say that Bach's music is only one of these tools, the purpose remaining the same.

As a requirement to reach Bach's peaks, one doesn't need to be a music professional, but a cultivated man, a man willing to evolve. The pieces of Bach's music that we like are also the ones we understand either because they are more accessible or because we are more spiritually advanced in that respect. In order to go forward with Bach's music we don't have to look for a formula, a helping equation that would decipher his works, but merely to feel in a superior way, to feel like Bach. For this, one should direct all his attention to more profound things, such as the soul and everything that is immaterial and spiritual in essence. Eventually, we can say that, as some religions state it, to some extent, this world is only a Great Illusion, but with consequences in the Real, Eternal World. So all we have to do is look for what is not an illusion, to look for the things that last, that remain, that have the certainty of absolute value.

Such a "great" feeling leads to a "great" understanding, and the enhanced understanding receives the gift and prize of the spiritual pleasure and teachings that Bach's music transmits. The "great" understanding can also be achieved by other field of knowledge and spirit.

J. S. Bach himself explained his music in the following words:
"The final ideal and purpose of the entire music should be no other than praising the Lord and delighting the soul."

Another great thinker, Plato, details more for us:
"Music is the movement of the sound to reach the soul for the education of its virtue." PLATO "The Republic"

In life, man must choose his way many times, but the most important choices he makes are the ones he makes without being asked to, the choices he wishes to be asked to make. Among these, there is the wish for perfection or the wish to meet the Creator. These simple, yet important wishes are at the origin of a complex and cultivated soul, as the very raison d'être of the soul, **its natural state**, is to saturate these wishes.

"Art would be useless if the world was perfect, for man wouldn't look for harmony, but would simply live in it." A. Tarkovsky

Art is the search for perfect harmony. Art exists only to educate man spiritually. But the first and cleanest educational tool, in terms of pragmatics, remains Theology. Art is not essential for spiritual education, as it only transmits, one way or another, the theological ideas, **the ideas that fix the world**. Theology is crucial, as it is the initiator of the ideas that bring perfection to man's life.

Nevertheless, Art has the advantage of facilitating man's meeting with the message of these ideas, especially in the case of those persons who don't necessarily look for the message and who are stricken (incited) by this message by means of the artistic object through which the message comes. When well shaped, the artistic object is able to create direct connections between man's soul and the divine energies that gave the harmony of Creation.

The purpose of art is harmony or, more precisely, seeing God by changing the glasses through which we look at His Creation. Each artist hands us **a set of glasses**, his art, and depending on the craftsmanship of these glasses, we, whether deeply educated or not, can see parts of Creation and pieces of God which we couldn't access before.

If we were to try to define the human culture in terms of God's gifts to artists, then we could say that it represents the sum of the human artistic activities that use God's gifts. Ultimately, culture is the sum of the effects of these gifts (which are the cause, originating directly in the Divinity) passed through the personal filter of each artist.

Since its cause has a divine origin (the gift), the effect of the gift (the artistic object) needs to be understood by considering the existence of God. If man (the channel) tries to interpret the cause (the gift, his art) through effects (artistic objects) separated from the divine meaning (artistic objects that deny the existence of God, either directly or through omission), then these effects are not only false and meaningless, spiritually illogical, but also an insult to the One who truly deserves the credit and the glory for them, as the One who lend the gifts to the artists.

Consequently, the artistic objects extract their value from their association with God's message to man.

This does not mean that the arts should deal exclusively with portraying God or with a kind of visual theology. The portrayal of Creation in all its forms and diversity is in itself a cataphatic theology (positive theology – God is in everything), knowing the Lord through the Creation in which He reversed His energies. Therefore, the man touched by the divine gift is free to move in the artistic space as he sees fit, but he can also apply the wise words of Saint Apostle Paul:

"All things are lawful for me, but all things are not expedient: all things are lawful for me, but all things edify not" 1 Corinthians 10, 23

Art does not contain the message, it merely expresses it through its various forms; but how soul-uplifting these forms are sometimes! Through its specific means, art brings man closer to the ardent sun of the theological ideas. For what is more ardent than God?

The Two Paths of the Search for Perfection

We often notice how a difference in quality is made in man's choice between the two roads proposed by the Church for man's perfection and union with God. The two roads are monasticism and laity. Bachelorhood, as life of an unmarried layman, is not a different path, but, if compliant with some basic rules of monasticism, it is then a different kind of monasticism with features of a lay life. If it does not comply with some basic monastic rules, like chastity, then it ceases to be a road to the Lord.

The two paths have their specific rules which, to a greater or lesser extent, cause the man who wishes to choose a way to fight a series of inner battles. Certainly, the decision in favor of one of the two paths is determined by the uniqueness of each person. Yet, unfortunately, most people have some preconceptions or spiritual gaps that influence the way they think which, in its turn, ends up influencing their decision which otherwise would have been different. Some of these preconceptions will be analysed here, but not all of them, as we are not omniscient and we cannot know and write everything on a given subject. Let us then analyse these errors one by one.

These preconceptions which we can say influence decisively any man who's on his way to know God are related to **the quality of the road**.

From the moment he was created, man was endowed with the wish to look for more quality in anything. We will now focus upon the wish for quality of the spiritual life. For the believer, the quality of the spiritual life is defined by how much he is united in his spirit with God, as a purpose of man's life.

The union with God is primordial in any decision that the believer will make even after he has chosen his path, but all the more so in the decision-making process for choosing a path.

One of the pro-monasticism arguments we hear from several sources is that this path is easier for searching the Lord.
And it really is, but only for those who go towards monasticism with a clear definition in their mind of

what they want from themselves. Monasticism is good only for those who have a vocation, not for the laymen who go to monasticism because of some physical, psychical or spiritual deficiencies or other problems.

Among the physical deficiencies invoked there are: lack of food, hard work, poverty, etc.

Among the psychical problems invoked there are: stress, inadaptation to the rules of society, lack of time for oneself because of the other members of society, lack of discipline, etc.

The spiritual wants referred to herein include the respective person's upsetting feeling that the world lacks spiritual peace and that the other people have no spiritual focus, etc.

These people have not examined enough the source of their problems and they try to solve them by taking the easier or the shorter way. For them, the wish to become a monk is not so much influenced by the quality of their spiritual life as by their negligence in dealing with their problems. They forget that, most times, these shortages were given by God Himself to put them to the test and, consequently, running away from them is not a solution. It didn't work for Prophet Jonah to run away, it will not work for them either.

A strong argument in favor of monasticism is that, in monasticism, a man interested in God can focus better on his search for God and on the spiritual life. This argument would be admissible if we assume that the man who makes the choice truly knows **why** he is interested in God and **he is interested for a real spiritual reason**. Man can be interested in God for reasons that only seem spiritual, but are in fact hidden passions; for example, those who look for God **to be happier** or those who look for Him **to know everything,** or those who look for the Lord because of an opportunistic fear of Hell. These people make the mistake of believing that the monastery is the place where they will find their fulfilment and then they are the ones disappointed that they haven't found in the monastery whatever it was they were looking for.

Certainly, everybody who goes to a monastery can be influenced by this spiritual environment and with a little spiritual education they could acquire a monastic vocation, singling themselves out from those who have chosen the wrong way. But it is equally true that this spiritual education is often not received by them, as they happen to lack a quality they didn't have even back in the world: obedience.

Another argument is of a pragmatic-spiritual nature. Why not try the safest way to redemption and be done with the small errors given by the other way?

All would be good if we knew what the best road for each of us is. But the truth is we don't know and those people who think they know and realize half-way that they don't know can have big problems on the road they have chosen. They would have been better off on the other road.

The worst is when they end up wishing they never made that choice and mistakenly fall into despair. Despair is a sin hard to bear. In general, it is the proud and falsely wise that bring this pragmatic-spiritual argument. After all, if the institution of monasticism did not exist, how would they manage? In fact, many prophets, apostles, righteous men and even our Lord, Jesus Christ, were not monks and lived in the world. To them, the institution of monasticism did not exist as we see it today. Naturally, many of them they lived as monks, but one could say just as well that they lived as laymen. For most people, the pragmatic-spiritual road is, in fact, a layman's life, as it has less strict spiritual rules than the life of a monk.

Another argument refers to the layman's way on his search for luxury and for an exaggerated quality of the material life.

Surely, for a monk with an advanced spiritual routine, how many or what kind of clothes he has in the closet would be of little if any interest. He would be pleased with only one plate for food and one spoon. He would by no means wish to change his furniture or see exotic or interesting places on earth. He may want to embark on one trip or two, as pilgrim, to some spiritual locations, but anything more than that would be unbecoming for him.

Things are different in a layman's life, given **his social relation to his fellow human beings and his responsibility towards his children**.

The layman tries to join his kind in order to share the Lord with them, or to rejoice with them with holy joy, or to accomplish a greater good with them.

So the layman has an obvious social responsibility. He needs clothes similar to the others, within reason, he needs a car or a fast means of transport so he can function socially at the pace required by modern society. He also needs a larger apartment or house, depending on his place in society and on what he is expected to be or to do in order to be accepted as a "normal" and "non-perverting" member of society or a show off like the Pharisee that though himself better than the tax collector.

Obviously, the layman should not abuse this wish for adaptability to society and, hence, fall into luxury, but neither should he catch people's eye by an exacerbated modesty whose effect, most times, whether with or without intent, is to rebuke the other people, maybe unjustly, without taking into account the condition of the people one wishes to admonish.

Apart from this, the layman, by the path he follows, has undertaken to a greater extent than the monk to study God's Creation and so he can use the tools which life in the world makes available to him. For example, if he wants to learn about animals, he can have access to modern equipment to study them: high-precision binoculars, professional cameras, video cameras, high-definition TV-sets, state-of-the art computers, etc. Although all of these and other objects may seem spiritually dangerous by their tendency towards luxury, in fact they don't have a bad influence on the layman's spiritual life, quite on the contrary. We can compare this to the situation where we hear the

Bible read by someone in a hoarse voice and we would like them to have a strong, clear voice. It is another form of wish for spiritual quality. For listening to classical music, one should have good and faithful interpretations, to listen to on high-definition equipment. Within a certain limit, this does not mean luxury, but taking what is needed to improve one's spiritual life. The Ecclesiast helps us with these words that show us what is good and beautiful in a layman's life to God's eyes:

"Behold, what I have seen to be **good and fitting** is to eat and drink and find enjoyment in all the toil with which one toils under the sun the few days of his life that God has given him, **for this is his lot**." The Ecclesiast 5, 18

The layman has the responsibility to procreate and to educate his children. Bringing as much quality as possible to these processes requires more material and psychic effort than if one didn't have children.

Sometimes, just ensuring the minimum quality to these processes (having and educating children) takes such a great effort that it can take all layman's free time and even most of its sleeping time. The monk does the easy part here, he only needs to take care of himself, to help taking care of other adults, and to educate, if possible, anyone who might need his spiritual help. The layman has full responsibility towards his children and he is not allowed or entitled to wait for any help from them until they are grown up and fully educated, so until the cycle of their formation as children has finished. Of course life is not perfect or ideal, but all men should aim for this.

Both the monk and the layman can look for God with the same spiritual intensity. Both paths have their specific traps and are perfectly equal in terms of chances for redemption. In the Egyptian hagiography, this question is answered by the response given to the question of Saint Anthony the Great who wanted to know if there was anyone else in this world able to reach his spiritual height. God showed him a **layman** in the nearest village, a man who had **the same spiritual height** as the great saint. The saint, who scared the devils with his saintly ascetic life, became humble. He wasn't better than next village guy.

The quality of the path is an argument only after man has made his choice and made it wisely. Not everybody can be a monk and not everybody should be a layman.

In the end, having and raising children is as important as personal redemption. It takes the same power of sacrifice and effort as personal redemption because the principles of success are the same. Consequently, what matters is not the path chosen in life, but its purpose. Man should keep in mind at all times the purpose of his path so as to avoid falling in the specific traps of the two roads and to reach the common purpose of both roads. And the purpose is to help man unite with God and, in his turn, help others join with Him.

Let us not judge the laymen or the monks. Let us thank God wherever and whatever we are and be sorrowful if we are not closer to Him.

The End of Catechisation

The Catechisation of the world, the moral teachings that help man going towards his God, that started at the same time with the creation of Adam is drawing to an end.

How do we know that? There are two ways in which a man can receive God's Word: with holy joy, because hearing the words that redeem everything fills the soul with joy, or with fight, as Cain became gloomy when he heard the Lord's word, advising him to overcome sin and join Him back.

Today we witness a fierce fight against all the moral values that the Lord's Word has given us throughout history. These days, more than in any other historical era after the coming of Christ, we get a feeling that the world hates to hear Christ's truth, namely the exhortation to turn our soul to our Heavenly Father. This is the sign that the teachings to the world reach their end and Catechisation will stop, as it is no longer welcome. These are the final steps of sifting the chaff from the wheat.

The believers start being attacked by the unbelievers. The spiritual values of the enemy, the Devil, start gaining momentum and push from the world psyche the Christian values as far away as they can, fighting to conquer as many souls as possible to take to eternal death. We hear more and more about the alteration of the natural order and about new ideas that try to reform the old (but not outdated) ideas of Christianity.

There was a time when the Christian ideas were deemed new and dangerous. Today, they are considered as completely known and **extremely dangerous**. The danger in the Christian ideas comes from the fact that the souls with Cain's attitude feel confronted by God's Truth, they hate the Light. It is without a doubt normal these days that these pagan souls rule the world. In any society, however good initially, the blood-shedders' ascent to power is merely a matter of time. The blood-shedders and the exploiters are "meant" to rule the world, because they are still allowed to do it so that the time of Judgement may come. By "meant", we should understand that they are the only ones who will wish and apply plans of deceit and brutality against those they want to rule. The other souls, not wanting to exploit their fellow human beings, will watch the exploiters do their way but will not interfere much, as the cup must be drunk to the bottom.

In other words, it's not yet the time to fight the enemy; after all, the believer knows that this fight will be fought by Christ Himself on His Second Coming and, so, believers will not take part in any plans of revenge or even violence against the exploiters, unless this violence is such that a Hero is desperately needed to bring back to men's souls the hope in God's values. Sometimes, divine values need our active protection if we want them to be heard again.

Catechisation, as a divine lesson will undoubtedly come to an end and it will come sooner than later, if we are to believe the word of God and judging be various signs. The time is drawing near when man will be received to the Father's right and will start his eternal relationship with the Father, consisting in his being taught by God.

This time though, after the Old World will pass, the teaching will no longer have the meaning of Catechisation, of a moral lesson, but of an everlasting explanation heartily wanted by the creature eager to know his Creator. That will be the time for living in God, in God's love, tête-à-tête, face to face, loving heart to loving eyes.

13

What is Man? And Why?

What is Man?
Is he a god?
Is he an angel?
Is he the Supreme Heir?

Is he a singular cell of "Alpha and Omega" (Revelation 12, 13) put in practice, the heights of heights to the infinite and the depths of depths to the infinite in the embryo stage? Why does he hold within the seed of unlimited power? Why does he hold within the wish for never-ending love? Why does Man feel he was not made to end in death or be limited by nothing and no one? Why does he think that God who made him, made man so as to be like Him in every aspect, only not to have omnipotence, but to look for it? Why was he given the wish to be fulfilled and completed with his God, which is impossible because God's Essence is inaccessible to him for eternity? Why was he given the hope that he will be for ever closer to God and, as such, closer to the qualities bestowed on him by this closeness?

Why was he, the creature created like the angels, given the taste of being a master of other creations, co-master with the Creator? Why was he given the gift of naming parts of the Creation? Doesn't naming mean finishing the Creation? Were the angels given the power and honor of naming something from the Creation? Why was man given the power of co-creating along with Love (God) other people and even to get an "ownership title" over some of the qualities of the future men created with his help - like family physiognomy?

Who else was given this grand destiny of completing Creation, apart from man and the One who controls his destiny? Others have tried to take God's power, but fell like flies, because the "air" they breathed was the Creator himself, whom they were going to fight… How is it possible that man is given, with God's permission, the status of Co-Master of the Creation elements and **even** the status of Co-Judge of the angels, God's most advanced creations? Who else but his Master and Heir can be the Judge? Who is the heir? Jesus, the man? Who/what is Jesus? Is he man? Is he God? Is he both?

How close can man get to God? What is the limit God imposed to man's ascent? Why is man left to know the deepest meanness and unholiness? Why is he left to know the blasphemy against the One who wants him to be His Co-Judge and Co-Master? Is this a kind of lesson in Power, Mastery and Judgement? Is this an attempt of humiliation, like an exercise of discipline (*"He who has never learned to obey cannot be a good commander."* Aristotle), so that man can afterwards appreciate the higher position? Who can judge besides the one who also has power, even if not originating in himself, but given to him by God?

Why is man not allowed to despair about his Salvation, however hurtful he may be to the Creation at some point in his life? Why is it that, WHATEVER man would do against God's Creation and even against God Himself, if man goes back to the Lord, everything will be forgiven to him and, with the divine permission and support, he will once again start his way to the heights and to judging God's Creation? Why weren't the fallen angels been given the same privilege? Are they less loved by the Lord, who is equal, non-discriminating Love?

What does man have so special deep down in his soul, put there by God, qualifying him for the honors that God willingly gives him? Who can judge someone who is his superior? Is man superior to the angels by divine choice? Aren't the angels God's messengers to **the other being (Man),** who is called to co-rule and co-judge with God? Is the angels' relationship with man a brotherly one or a subordinate one? Are the angels the future subordinates of men, subject to their judgement, as suggested by Apostle Paul?

Why aren't the angels the first in line? Why are men? Why did God choose to have a form and he wished that form to be human for eternity? What is Man? How is Man like? Who is Man?

Man, the being whom God gave Himself to in order to be eaten alive - The Sacrament of the Eucharist.

Man, the being worthy enough to eat and drink God's flesh and blood (see John 6, 53-58).

Man, becoming God by taking over in his body God's Image, through the deification process laid out for him by God.

God's words towards Man in Eden:

"Fill the earth and **subdue it**." Genesis 1, 28

„**Rule** over the fish in the sea and the birds in the sky and over every living creature that moves on the ground." Genesis 1, 28

"It is not good that the man should be alone; I will make him a help **suitable** for him." Genesis 2, 18

"But for Adam there was not found a help **suitable** for him. And the Lord God caused a deep sleep to fall upon the man, and he slept; and He took one of his ribs, and closed up the place with flesh instead thereof. And **the rib, which the Lord God had taken from the man, made He a woman, and brought her unto the man**." Genesis 2, 20-22

"And out of the ground the Lord God formed every beast of the field, and every fowl of the air; and brought them unto the man to see what he would call them; **and whatsoever the man would call every living creature, that was to be the name thereof.** And the man gave names to all cattle, and to the fowl of the air, and to every beast of the field." Genesis 2, 19-20

God's words towards Man after Eden:

"Today you will be with me in Paradise." Luke 23, 43

"We shall judge angels." 1 Corinthians 6, 3

"You will see the Son of Man sitting at the right hand of the Mighty One" Mark 14, 62

"The Father judges no one, but has entrusted all judgement to **the Son**;" John 5, 22

"And hath given **him** authority to execute judgment also, **because he is the Son of Man.**" John 5, 27

PART II

"Let there be light!"

Genesis 1,2

Questions regarding the Genesis

Question 1:

1:2. *"Let there be light! And there was light."*

This was made in day one. It seems to say that the sun was created, as only the sun can make the difference between light and darkness.

On the other hand, verse 16 reads:

"And God made two great lights: the greater light to rule the day..."

These luminaries were created in day four. It seems to mean that the sun was created. Again ?!?

Sometimes, it looks as if God wishes to puzzle His apologists, to test their faith. Even a man with limited knowledge thinks based on the cause-and-effect principle. If the light appeared before the luminaries, it is obvious that we have such a big problem that it becomes silly! We could even say that someone had us sell a product they designed badly on purpose to laugh at our attempts at selling it. Or is this all a test of faith?

In fact, reality is sheer beauty: God is efficient. God wants to teach us not only that He is the cause of all things, but more than that. The entire chapter of Genesis consists of material terms: He did that, He created the other, this thing appeared, etc. But the way in which the creations are put there makes us rather think about what God wanted from His creation. It arouses our interest. After all, He could have created the world in a nanosecond (some say He actually did – see the Bing-Bang theory), he didn't need 7 days, which can also be interpreted as billions of years.

The light appeared before the luminaries, because the temporal and physical luminaries do not give out "light", they give out radiations, which, after all, are material particles. It is the Holy Spirit who gives out light.

The light of God is not physical, although it can cross the physical spectrum, meaning it can be seen materially, as well, with God's will. Examples: the burning bush (there were no physical flames, although they could be seen); the death of Sisoes, the monk in the Egyptian hagiography who filled his cell with a blinding light, coming from his face, as a reflection of what he then saw, just like the moon is lighted by the sun and, in its turn, reflects its light. But Saint Sisoes's face did not reflect any source of radiations (material luminaries), but the light of the Lord, as the prophets and the Saviour Himself had come to welcome his passage to death. Another example is Saint Seraphim of Sarov, who lighted a whole meadow with his body in the middle of the night for the engineer Motovilov, thus showing he was full of the Holy Spirit and, as such, of the light of God. Last, but not least, the example of our Saviour on Mount Tabor, where the light that sprang from His body made the apostles John and Peter bow to earth, to protect their eyes from the light of God , a spiritual light, also visible in the material space.

It is this light that the Genesis 1, 3 speaks of. The light of the Holy Spirit reflected in the material world: the light of God. After this, He made the luminaries, but they were merely radiation with material purposes. The light comes from somewhere else.

Another interesting question arises from the first days of Genesis, when, on day three, **before the**

creation of the luminaries, something even more illogical happens:

"And God said: "Let the earth sprout vegetation, plants yielding seed, and fruit trees bearing fruit in which is their seed, each according to its kind, on the earth". And it was so." Genesis 1, 11

What kind of light warmed and lighted the grass and fruit trees? The light of the Holy Spirit.! Great mystery! God makes the rules of the game and He can change them any time, at the beginning of Creation, in its middle or in its twilight.

Question 2:

1:24. "Let the earth bring forth living creatures according to their kinds - livestock and creeping things and beasts of the earth according to their kinds."

So the wild animals were created wild, they did not become so after a certain event, is that true?

"Beasts of the earth" does not mean that they were not friendly towards Man, but that they were "free" animals, which is the opposite of "livestock", of serving somebody, through conditioning. Try conditioning with a tiger and see what is happening. Sure, for a while he can play along... but do not get fooled.

After the Fall of Man some animals, like livestock, were chosen to continue their respect for Man and thus become tameable, so he can still feel their love for him, to continue his relationship with them, while wild animals were chosen to show God's punishment to Man and thus they become unruly, untameable, disobedient from their former master, Adam, as Adam was disobedient from God.

The so-called wild or free animals did not eat each other, or getting ruff with each other in the Garden of Eden, but they weren't man's slaves there either. They were not bound to do as he pleased, as he did with the tameable ones, which after the Fall of Man sometimes was to kill or torture them and force them to work. He was their master by Will of God and in the Garden of Eden the untameable animals along with the tameable ones showed Man the consideration due to a superior being, but without losing their dignity, as wild and untameable animals do today, when they either show consideration out of fear only or they don't show any consideration at all, losing their dignity by dichotomy with man, their master, fighting each other when it is the case.

We see in the Church Fathers' histories cases of "wild" animals that behaved with dignity and humility at the same time; for example, the case of an old man served and buried by a lion. That lion was free, "wild" but also he behaved like in the Garden of Eden, by will of God, even if it lived after the event of the Fall of Man.

The wolf is like an untameable dog, but the wolf can **become friends** with man, just like in the beginning of their relation in Eden, without ever becoming a servile or tamed animal. Friendship is different from obedience in the sense that friendship is more than obedience. It is more profound in its inner works.

Man's sin has affected the entire Nature in the mysterious way chosen by God so that, according to God's plan, even the punishment may teach and correct. This is why, after the Fall of Man wild animals eat each other and us... with exceptions. They are the expression of the discord between Man and God and so, between Man and Nature - God's creation.

Some animals were chosen to serve man after the Fall of Man. Thus, some of them, on a case by case basis, were endowed by God with the trait of **tamableness**, although all their species are free at origin. They obey God's will and, due to this duty, they reach high levels of dignity.

Let us not forget God's pre-cognition: as a Being that lives outside of Time, God foresaw the Fall of Man, and the Creation became functional or kept its functionality even after this destructive event, also due to the God's pre-cognition and anticipation of the post-Fall period.

We see in the Holy Scripture, Isaiah 65, 25 that the wolf sat with the lamb:

> *"The wolf and the lamb shall graze together; the lion shall eat straw like the ox, and dust shall be the serpent's food. They shall not hurt or destroy in all my holy mountain", says the LORD".*

Although the verse speaks about the future or maybe it also has another, more spiritual meaning, we can understand from it that, in the beginning, the Lord did not create the lion to eat meat or the wolf to eat lambs. Just like man did not eat just anything back then, the way he does today with animals, including eating other people. This is why the Lord, after looking at His Creation, considered that everything was **"very good"**. For, if there had been anything deemed harmful after seven days of Creation, He would not have thought it all "very good". If the animals had ripped each other apart, in a death orgy (death did not exist yet, so they did not die in Eden), than He would have definitely thought this was bad and harmful.

In fact, in Eden there was no pain, no accidents, because all the living beings were watched over through the Holy Spirit. For example, if your foot slipped, you couldn't fall and break your hip, or, even if you fell, you didn't get injured. Or you just didn't fall and none of the disagreeable trifles of today happened back then. There was no sadness, either, because they were all connected to the Lord, the source of happiness and spiritual, hence, emotional fulfilment.

Apart from this, the animals had additional attributes or they were perfect. For example, birds sang without flaw. The flaw exists because of physical causes, i.e. the muscles are not perfectly coordinated to give out a proper trill, or it is too cold and the vocal chords are injured.

Certainly, some will say that the polar bear and the penguin would have had great difficulties in sharing the same place or climate with the desert lion. But who knows the conditions in which the lions or the polar bears lived back then? All we know is that they did not suffer from the temperature, either, because they were much more adaptable or because God took care that they feel perfectly in any climate or temperature.

Other examples in recent history of God's temperature tolerant experiments:

- The Lord keeps in optimum living conditions the three young men thrown by Nebuchadnezzar in the hot oven;

- One can feel cold, or hot or comfortable in the same given temperature.

In conclusion, everything was possible in the Garden of Eden, even a bank of snow that could not be melted by the burning sun. After all, this is possible at the zoo nowadays, and we don't claim to be almighty.

God's miracles are varied, which means that things in the Garden of Eden could be as God wanted them to be, and not only in one way, but in various ways, one more wonderful and unthinkable for these days than the other.

Question 3:

The Book of Genesis 2:10-14 describes the river that watered the Garden of Eden and the four heads that parted from it: Pison (the country of Havilah), Gihon (the country of Cush), Tigris (Assyria), and Euphrates. The conclusion is that Eden was on Earth, as were the Tree of Life and the Tree of Knowledge between Good and Evil. If it does not exist anymore, has the geographical structure of the area changed dramatically in time or does it refer to an area that is not located on Earth?

3:24 "He drove out the man, and at the east of the garden of Eden he placed the cherubim and a flaming sword that turned every way to guard the way to the tree of life."

Is Eden still on Earth nowadays?

Eden was created on Earth before the Fall of Man and it remained there even after that terrible event. This is known for sure as, right after the Fall of Man, God had to place the Cherubim with flaming swords at its entries (which could be anywhere) in order to keep away Adam or the beings cast out of Eden. God put Adam "around the Garden of Eden" to work the land and to have visual access to what he had lost because of his disobedience.

After a while, Eden was hidden from the eyes of men. This may have happened in Adam's time or afterwards and it may still be revealed to deserving eyes. It has not stopped existing. It is certain that, by Noah's time, it was already hidden, because men no longer believed in God. They had no physical, graphical, touchable proof of His perfection, but merely of His power, which was the world – the wild nature we live in today, but which they chose to consider as a world without a Creator, as it happens these days, as well. If men could see Eden today with their own eyes, even from afar, then they would no longer question the existence of the Perfect Being, they would have the proof of His existence and, at the same time, they would regain their life purpose: getting back to Eden. But, for many, Eden would be a selfish/opportunistic purpose, which is a wrong purpose in spiritual terms.

The purpose of man's life is to be "in the Lord" and not to selfishly enjoy what the Lord can give, wanting the gifts more than the Lord Himself. The first question to ask a man who is interested in the Lord is "Why are you interested in the Lord?". And if the answer is more or less along the lines of "I'm waiting for alms", then we'll know we're dealing with a lazy beggar.

There is a reference in the book of Leimon - "Spiritual Meadow" - written by John Moschus in 7th century about something that happened to a monk in the 4th century. This monk lived in a monastery and, one day, as he was in the woods, he saw and listened to a bird from Eden. After he listened to the bird in awe, he rushed to the monastery to share this with his fellow monks. But when he got there he knew nobody and nobody knew him. After a long research of the monastery books, they found that a monk with his name had lived 300 years before their time and one day had disappeared. The new monks lived in the seventh century. The monk told them what had happened to him, said a prayer and yielded up his soul, with God's will.

This teaches us that Eden still exists and is still populated by some of God's creatures.

Question 4:

3:1. "Now the serpent was more crafty than any other beast of the field which the Lord God had made."

The serpent is called a beast on earth. According to tradition, the serpent is Satan. If we refer to Satan, this means that Satan was already on earth at the time of the discussion between the Serpent and Eve. Tradition also teaches us that Satan was thrown down to earth, along with a third of the angels, after their riot against God.

In conclusion, Satan was already in conflict with God when he tempted Eve?

Satan was indeed already in conflict with God when he tempted Adam and Eve. But the Book of Genesis does not give any specific details about his fall since all the Books of the Bible are part of a message to Man and less directed to angels. We don't see the chronology or the manner in which **all the events** have occurred from the beginning until these days, just like we don't know EVERYTHING that happens on Earth every day, every second, to be able to draw conclusions in any subject matter. This is why they say sometimes

"Believe and don't doubt", because of the lack of all the facts. In fact, man could not receive the data even if they were accessible to him because Man was not created omniscient. Additional information can be given to him through the Holy Spirit, only by God's will, so you do not need to just believe without proof, but to ask for further spiritual data, and until you receive what you ask, you are required to not doubt the Word of the Lord.

Naturally, Gods' Will can be influenced. We know that because of this permission: *"Ask and it will be given to you"* (Mathew 7, 7). In general, the preliminary condition for us to learn as many spiritual things as possible including the events and their explanation is spiritual cleanliness. Otherwise, nobody will cast *"pearls before swine"* (Mathew 7, 6).

Satan was in conflict to God since he was first touched by Pride, shortly after all Creation was finished. One chronological indication that his fall was before the Fall of Man is that he tempted Man and lied to him. What angel of God will do such a thing to the less endowed Man?

However, when he was created and during all seven days of creation he was good, as seen in God's remark about all things being "very good" right after finishing Creation.

Something happened immediately after Creation that made Satan turn bad. John 3, 8 confirms this by saying *"the devil has been sinning since the beginning"*.

As we know Lucifer, "the morning star" was created more beautiful than others and he was kept closer to God's throne than others, as stated by Ezekiel 28, 12: *"You were the seal of perfection, Full of wisdom and perfect in beauty"*. He was a Cherub with more power and more spiritual responsibility to protect Creation than all the other "morning stars". As seen here: *"You were the anointed cherub who covers; I established you; You were on the holy mountain of God; You walked back and forth in the midst of fiery stones."* Ezekiel 28, 14

But most important than anything Satan was **Perfect**, so with no right to desire more: *"You were perfect in your ways from the day you were created, Till iniquity was found in you."* Ezekiel 28, 15

We see him performing his duties in a very professional manner but already with a hidden agenda in the Story of Job, where he plays the role of the Accuser, but not because he wanted to protect Gods creation, but because he was already against God Himself and as such, against everything that God created. We see here how *"the Father of Lies"* (John 8, 44) lies first to himself when he thinks he is improving Creation by destructive justice.

God plays along just to show Satan that he is wrong about Job and also to give Satan a chance to learn from Job, who was just a man.

Job chose God against the wisdom of his loving friends. That story shows us **that even Wisdom is not a protection against falling to sin**, because Job's friends were wise. Job chose God against what he perceived as utterly unfair treatment from God. God was more important to Job than whatever God gave him to please him or even to torture him. Job was the Lesson for Satan. That is the only reason God let Satan touch everything he had but Job's life. Job had the right attitude and as such, he made the correct "offering" to God as **"righteous Abel"** (Matthew 23, 35) did before him.

So Perfection and Wisdom is not to be desired beyond all measure as they cannot protect against error and failure. The right "offering" is written more plainly here: *"The sacrifices of God are a broken spirit. A broken and a contrite heart, These, O God, You will not despise."* Psalm 51, 17

The reason for this is that we and even the angels are not All-Knowing. And to be able to survive in God's Creation you either need to be All-Knowing yourself or if you are not, then the only chance you have is to give yourself and all your actions to the only All-Knowing Being out there. God gives you the choice, the free-will, out of Love for you. There are however an infinite number of wrong choices. But there is only one good choice.

Did Satan learn from Abel? Did he learn from Job? Does he learn from the choice of all the martyrs?

The great lesson here is that perfection is not the ultimate state in which you are protected of committing sin. Because even when you have everything it means nothing without God:

"Your heart was lifted up because of your beauty; **You corrupted your wisdom for the sake of your splendor.**" Ezekiel 28, 17

All our actions, thoughts included, as immaterial actions, needs to be done for the sake of God. And in that we shall find the correct choice, **the correct "offering"**.

Question 5:

3:14. "Because you have done this, cursed are you above all livestock and above all beasts of the field; on your belly you shall go, and dust you shall eat all the days of your life."

God's curse against the snake does not seem to be cast at Satan, but at the animal. The animal has a finite life – see the sub-paragraph "all the days of your life". Tradition tells us that Satan and his angels are immortal beings and, as such, it cannot be said that the days of their life are numbered. If this hypothesis is correct, how did the snake talk to Eve?

The snake spoke through the will-power of Satan. Similarly to the other animals, the snake was not created with reason. So he did not speak by himself, but contributed to this. He gave his acceptance just like we tacitly accept something without speaking or thinking. Hence his error: he contributed to ruining the harmony between Eve and himself by working with the Evil one against her. In other words, he initiated the challenge by collaborating with Satan to act against God's will.

In Eden, all the animals had the possibility to obey or not to obey the Lord. The snake chose not to obey, thus collaborating to a deed contrary to the divine will. We can also see he had a choice from the fact that God punishes him. For, if it had not been in his power to choose, then God would have considered him blameless and God does not punish innocents. Will God even talk to an animal if that animal cannot feel his Will or make personal choices concerning God's Will, like we do?

Also, as far as animal speaking is concerned, the history of humanity has witnessed at least one more animal that spoke intelligibly, not like the parrots. One such example is the donkey of Balaam as seen in Numbers 22, 27-30, and again in 2 Peter 2, 16.

The important aspect here is that God also was the one that let the snake speak, as he did not interfered with the mischievous plans of Satan, since both Satan and Eve had freewill. So when Satan wanted to use the snake to tempt Eve, God let it happen so that Man's obedience is tested accordingly to God's Plans. The conversation between Snake-Satan and Eve is important in history because all parties wanted to happen: Satan (angels), Eve (humans) and God.

It is not only a test for Eve but mainly for Satan, who pushed further his rebellion with this second act following the first act of Pride. God is assured now that Satan wants to alter His Creation one way or another. Eve also accepted to talk with the snake because she wanted a different opinion than God's opinion, since it was Him who gave the command that the fruits should not be eaten. So she was happy to talk with the snake and it trusted him, as nothing bad ever happened, so she didn't know that Evil existed already right there close to her in the form of a snake possessed by Satan.

Of course, once the snake tried to make a liar out of God, Eve could easily back off his proposal of disobedience, but this is the moment that shows us that disobedience was already a disposition that Eve acquired, maybe even at the moment she found out about the Command not to touch those fruits. The disastrous consequences of a disobedient human heart, helped by a disobedient angel's advice are seen now throughout our entire history. And throughout all history, God is still trying to teach us the safety and naturalness of an obedient heart.

Question 6:

3:15. "And I will put enmity between you and the woman, and between your offspring and her offspring; he shall bruise your head, and you shall bruise his heel."

It looks like a reference to the conflict between the seed of the serpent, the son of the snake, the son of Satan, the Antichrist and...

This is the first prophecy about the salvation of Man through the Messiah, the Son of Man and it was address to Satan. It establishes the fact that the Messiah will come through a woman and will be a man and that He will destroy Satan's power. The prophecy also establishes that the Messiah will suffer because of Satan, which did happen through His public opprobrium and crucifixion. Through the apostles and saints that followed, we can see how Satan's power over men, passions, sins, was crushed: the saints became free from Original Sin through the power of the Messiah (one becomes free from the Original Sin through the Sacrament of Baptism) and they stayed free from Passions through the power of the Holy Spirit with the help given by the Sacrament of Confession, and the

Sacrament of the Holy Communion, free from the Original Sin and free from Passions being two different thing. The prophecy has already been fulfilled through Jesus Christ and it keeps being fulfilled every day, since the Resurrection of the Lord and until the end of the world.

The crushing of the serpent's head seems related to the danger of having one's heel stung by its venomous teeth. Therefore, this is a courageous, heroic act, full of love and sacrifice for the people that you want to save from the snake. Thus, this verse also shows us that the Messiah and everybody that associates with Him will suffer **during** the act of crushing of Satan's power, but that in the end He will be victorious. **The cross** was both this suffering and a symbol of the crushing of Satan. This is why the cross is "the heel" with which we must step on earth each day, "the heel" that crushed Satan and his plans to enslave the entire humankind. The death of Christ on the Cross and His Resurrection are the only historical events that give man hope against Satan's power.

Of course, not all people decide to take advantage of the fact that the Lord made us free from sin or that He brought us the path to God. But this does not mean that the prophecy has not been and is not fulfilled every day.

Our life is a test for each and every one of us and we know our two choices: either with God's Will or against it.

Question 7:

After Adam and Eve had children, how did the species perpetuate considering that, according to the information in the Holy Scripture, there were no other people than Adam, Eve and their children?

"The days of Adam after he fathered Seth were eight hundred years: and he had other sons and daughters."
Genesis 5, 4

Before Seth, naturally, ever since Adam had Abel and Cain, he also had daughters; proof of this is that Cain was banished along with his woman, one of his sisters.

These sons and daughters procreated other sons and daughters. Consequently, the brothers and sisters procreated, later on, so did first cousins and, afterwards, more and more distant cousins. This was way back, when procreation was not used as a channel for perversion or, more precisely, for subduing the other, when it was not used to gather or to show off power.

The world got dirty little by little, just like the long-lasting cleaning process takes place gradually.

God began to give the world "healing laws", among the first ones being those that forbade procreation with persons with direct or second grade blood connections: daughters or 1st grade cousins.

These girls were too exposed to the parental or brotherly abuse to develop in a decent way as wife. The two kinds of love they knew – the love of a father and brother, and the love of a husband – needed to be strictly differentiated, and not merged by the same persons who gave them life and offered them their first protection in life. Consequently, they began to be protected by the "specific law", given by revelations or directly by God to the righteous men and the patriarchs of the time, who taught the people by means of words and deeds, and not merely by the "law of nature", contained in men's souls and stressed by their conscience. The "specific law" also established the connections between the future bride and groom and even the connections between the bride and the father-in-law so that all involved could be protected by abuse or misdirection.

These laws were told to the world, first to the patriarchs, who then taught them orally to the others, when the healing process began. But at the beginning of man's life on earth, when people were much cleaner, these specific laws had no object, as people were not pervert and did not abuse. Everything took place naturally and the law of nature sufficed.

Certainly, this period of semi-cleanliness did not last very long.

Thus, gradually, God began to punish people, first by shortening their life (*"And the LORD said: My spirit shall not abide in man forever, for he is flesh: his days shall be a hundred and twenty years"* Genesis 6, 3) and then, when they became unbearable to look at and totally unrepentant, by sending the Flood over them. By the time of Noah, people were as debauchee as they could be, so the Flood was the only option to start over clean, choosing the ONLY family that remained in obedience to God to recommence Man's road to redemption.

The specific laws were given by the Holy Spirit to the patriarchs and to the sons of God, so the spiritual healing process started first through the patriarchs and the sons of God.

Not all of God's sons listened to these laws, as most of them fell to the daughters of men and listened to their ways, according to Genesis 6, 2: *"The sons of God saw that the daughters of men were attractive; and they took as their wives any they chose."*.

The sons and daughters of God were from the seed of Set, not from that of Cain, which gave the sons and daughters of man. In time, some of God's sons, who did not fall, received laws through the Holy Spirit. So the Holy Spirit taught them, through his methods: inspiration, revelation, epiphany, visions, and words actually heard or only known in their hearts.

Eventually, the laws were exposed in a more elaborate manner and with the indisputable authority of God's thunder-like voice in the time of Moses on Mount Sinai. Then these laws were completed by Jesus Christ, by the apostles and, finally, by the Christian bishops through the laws of the church. But all of these "modern" laws were made legitimate through the Holy Spirit, left by Jesus on Pentecost Day.

The Holy Spirit legitimizes the new laws through the previously given laws which, sometimes paradoxically, even when they contradict each other, reveal a higher and more profound look over God's plan for man's redemption. For example when Jesus is asked in relation to Moses divorce procedure, He revealed that it is not a perfect procedure, but one that was given to men at some point in history based on the wisdom of their hearts, or to be more precise, the lack of it (see Mathew 19, 3-9).

Question 8:

4: "But for Cain and his offering he had no regard. And Cain was very angry, and his face fell.

The Lord said to Cain: Why art you angry and why has your face fallen? If you do well, will you not be accepted? And if you do not do well, sin is couching at the door. Its desire is for you, but you must rule over it!"

The underlying meaning here is that, if sin knocks at the door, if the devil tempts us to do evil things, we should resist and conquer it. But what was Cain's fault that made God not like his offering? Why does He say "If you do well, will you not be accepted"?

Is this the same as saying: when you know that you have done your job well, as well as you can, and that you can't do any better than that, we are serene because we are at peace with ourselves knowing we can't do any better? If Cain offered a sizable offer from his goods, as Abel did from his own, than why God was not content with Cain's Offer?

Cain's face had fallen under the burden of his sin and not because of God's reaction to his offering.

This can be seen from Cain's reaction: instead of asking the Lord why He didn't like his offering, he becomes gloomy and keeps the reason of his sadness to himself. This happens because his reason, also known by the Lord, is his sin against God's will, disobedience of the Lord, as life principle. The Lord tries to pull Cain from the revolt and the despair brought along by his sin. This is a true revolt because Cain wishes the sin and as such he does not like God's Rule, and he despairs because he knows that his will is against the divine will and he has no chance to argue reasonable in favor of keeping the pleasure he takes in the sin of disobedience, the mindless freedom he experience.

The Lord tries to bring Cain back on track, back to the life purpose of becoming better, of doing good things all the time, of constantly improving himself through his love for God, of eventually becoming one with God. But Cain loves the sin and the only method of giving it up successfully is the one he doesn't see: loving God more and giving up sin not in order to observe God's will, out of fear, but to fulfill the divine will out of love. In fact,

God gives Cain a way by which to praise Him: by loving Him and by doing good things out of love for the Lord.

Cain understands or more correctly said, he wants to understand ONLY the respect of power, which comes from fear of the other's power, because he, too, wants the same relationship with the surrounding world: a relationship based on the hierarchy of power. In other words: I have my own boss (God) and I can't help that, but I am your boss and you'll do what I say or else you will suffer under my power... We can see that from two events described in the Genesis:

1. When the Lord asks Cain about Abel's whereabouts, Cain replies that Abel is not part of the responsibilities the Lord gave him, that he is not one of the things or beings assigned to him to rule. In other words, his brother is not given to him to control as he want it, so this is a worldview that show a structure of responsibility based on power and not of love.

   The correct answer would have been that all beings, humans or animals, are Cain responsibility, but not to order them around and abuse them, but to protect, help and love them.

2. When the Lord shows him that Abel acted right before Him, Cain thinks in terms of competitiveness and hierarchy of power and tries to usurp Abel's first place by killing him, as the mobsters or politicians do, in order to physically take his place, not thinking about how God's harmonious Creation might be affected by this monstrous act. In Cain's mind, if the first place disappears, he would rise from the second place to the first one.

The correct way of thinking would have been to take Abel's example, as from someone more enlightened by the Holy Spirit and to ask Abel how to present his offering to the Lord, so that the Lord would like the offering and more importantly, He will like Cain's attitude.

But Cain **does not want** to have a relationship with the Lord. He tries to tolerate God in his life, just because of His power. This is also why his offering is made with a heavy heart and rebellion.

This is the **key reason** why people today have their life led by sin: they willingly and purposefully separate themselves from God. Most people today are not ignorant in their relation with God, but wholeheartedly wish to separate themselves from Him.

Cain is upset because, from his point of view, he made his offering, which he considers "the percentage of respect" required and God should be pleased as, in quantitative terms, he took all the measures for God to be satisfied. But the Lord, who created everything, among which Cain's offering, too, already has it all, so the offering made by Cain is an insult to Him because of what this offer **means** to Cain. The Lord shows in the Psalms, which are the Holy Spirit's words in the mouth of the prophet, the offering He wished from Cain and from anyone else:

"For you will not delight in sacrifice, or I would give it; you will not be pleased with a burnt offering. The sacrifices of God are a broken spirit; a broken and contrite heart, O God, you will not despise." Psalm 51, 16-17

Cain's sin is **the wish for power**, and the righteous path required by God is **the wish for love of God**. Depending on this decision, man's life, like that of Cain will go up or down on the ladder of vices and virtues.

The measure by which we can measure our road to God is given by this passage in the Epistle I John, Chapter 3:

*"For this is the message that you have heard from the beginning, that **we should love one another**. We should not be like Cain, who was of the evil one and murdered his brother. And why did he murder him? Because his own deeds were evil and his brother's righteous. Do not be surprised, my brothers, if the world hates you. We know that we have passed from death to life, because we love our brothers. Anyone who does not love remains in death. Anyone who hates his brother is a murderer, and you know that no murderer has eternal life in him."* 1 John 3, 11-15

Question 9:

6:2. *"The sons of God saw that the daughters of man were attractive. And they took as their wives any they chose.*

3. Then the LORD said, "My Spirit shall not abide in man forever, for he is flesh: his days shall be 120 years."

4. The Nephilim (giants) were on the earth in those days, and also afterward, when the sons of God came in to the daughters of man and they bore children to them. These were the mighty men who were of old, the men of renown."

Is it possible that the Nephilim, the giants are the offspring of women and the third part of the angels banished on earth?

The Nephilim are not the offspring of any angels, whether good or bad, with women. Angels cannot copulate with women, as they are spirits without body. Nevertheless, they can possess people. And by possessing people, they can end up copulating, but the children resulting from this copulation still could not be called children of angels, but merely children of possessed people, who inherit the sins of their parents, not those of the angels.

The sons of God are the descendants of Seth, who have remained faithful to the Lord. They are sons of God both due to their genealogy and spiritual choice of being faithful to God only. They are sons of God through the grace received by Seth as a patriarch, and due to his obedience to God's laws.

The Nephilim are mainly the result of the joining between the sons of God and the daughters of men. The sons of God had qualities which we would nowadays call superhuman. We don't know all of them, but we know that they lived long, they were intelligent and strong. The Bible specifies "in those days" as a time when the giants existed but it also adds this detail: "and also afterword", which seem to show that Nephilim were born even before the sons of God fall with daughters of men. From this we see that they are most likely a "gift" to the sons of God than a consequence of these sons going with the fallen daughters of men. This gift consists in giving special abilities or stature to the children of the son of God. However, as with any powerful gift, it comes with great responsibility. The Giants started to think of themselves as more important than the average men, and under their leadership men went against God's will, as seen from the poor state of the world, just before the Flood.

To see some of the Nephilim's gifts we have to look at their parents before the Flood and some of their descendents after the Flood.

An example of intelligence and great strength is Noah, a Patriarch and a son of God, who built the huge arc only with his arms and those of his family.

An example of incredible size and strength is shown in the descendants of Anak as described in Numbers 13, 32-33. Other known giants after the Flood are Goliath and King Og of Bashan.

In terms of longevity, all the patriarchs are an example and it is logical that their children be given a long life, as well, so that they may all rejoice together, along with their sons, grand children, great-grand-children and their children for hundreds of years. Family reunions were a true blessing of God for them.

Let us now analyse an interesting aspect that reveals us more about the sons of God. As we can see in 6:2, God reduces the life of the sons of God who took daughters of men as their wives down to approximately

120 years. This started to happened back in the time of Noah, before the Flood and continued after the Flood. But this limitation did not affect the Patriarchs and some of their children. Thus, according to Genesis chapter 11, Shem lived for 600 years, Arpachshad 460 years, Cainan years 460, Shelah 460 years, Eber 504 years, Peleg 339 years, Rehu 339 years, Serug 230 years, Nahor 148 years, Terah 205 years and then Abraham 175 years while his wife Sarah lived 127 years, Isaac 180 years and Jacob 147 years, the last of the Patriarchs. Interesting to know is that Moses lived exactly 120 years, the limit which God imposed to men as opposed to the sons of God. Of course that some people may live a few years above this limit by the grace of the Lord, but that does not change the upper limit of about 120 years that we see in our modern lives.

We should also understand that the sons of men, starting with Cain, began to live contrary to God's will in almost all the aspects of their life. For example, we can imagine that Cain's relation to his women was different in terms of respect from Seth's relation to his women. The same goes for the "political" aspect for the men under Cain, who had a relation based on power and gangster-ism, compared to the relation with the men under Seth, relation based on the patriarch's authority given by the Lord. The former learn a set of values brought by the advice of the lying, manipulative devil, and the latter a set of values taught directly by God.

The joining of the sons of God with the daughters of men, who were pagan, since they were alienated from God, merged a few qualities and parameters of both kinds of people, but no values. The sons of God who joined the daughters of men lost the status of sons of God and a large part of the qualities they had before, including their age that was limited down to 120 years, which the sons of God, who did not fall from grace kept.

Wisdom was the first thing that the fallen sons of God lost, along with the True Sight, through the Holy Spirit, of the world and the entire creation around it, both physical, the Universe and the forces within it and spiritual, the world of the angels and talking to God.

This is one of the reasons for which they no longer saw Eden, which was still on earth. Hence, their increasing lack of faith in God's presence and miracles.

Question 10:

9:2. "The fear of you and the dread of you shall be upon every beast of the earth and upon every bird of the heavens, upon everything that creeps on the ground and all the fish of the sea. Into your hand they are delivered."

So is the relation with the animals based on fear and hierarchy, according to God's word?

Man's sin affected the entire nature, in the way chosen by the Lord, so that, according to God's plan, even the punishment would teach and remedy. This is why wild animals eat each other and us... with exceptions: their criminal attitude is the effect of the discord between man and God, of man's banishment from Eden.

In Eden, God made Man and animals vegetarian: *" And God said, "Behold, I have given you every plant yielding seed that is on the face of all the earth, and every tree with seed in its fruit. You shall have them for food. And to every beast of the earth and to every bird of the heavens and to everything that creeps on the earth, everything that has the breath of life, I have given every green plant for food." And it was so."* Genesis 1, 29

The fear and dread come from the law given by God **after** the fall from Eden:

*"Every moving thing that lives shall be food for you. And **as I gave you the green plants**, I give you everything."* Genesis 9, 3

So, before the Fall of Man, the animals were safe, mastered by man, but loved, protected and understood. After the Fall of Man, they were hunted, tortured, and not understood. They lost their **Master**, the man from Eden, who loved and protected them, and they were handed over to **the new ruler**, the fallen, corrupted man, who would hunt and eat them. Fear also comes from not understanding the partner's intentions. The understanding between animals and man disappeared, the communication channel was destroyed. A similar thing happened in the Babel Tower, where not only the common language disappeared, but the unity of thought, as well. For, if only the language had changed, people would have continued to build the tower, even if they had been forced to communicate by signs. This is why prayers are important for the unity. The ideological split, the lack of unity of thought leads to disaster.

Consequently, man's relationship with the animals in Eden relied on respect and love. Life in Eden would not have allowed fear and dread as natural life quality standards there. The animals were not created to receive from God as "gift", fear and dread.

"Fear and dread" came after the Fall of Man. The words in Genesis 9:2 refer to man's new relation with the animals. Here already, with these words, we enter the part of history where it becomes clear that a process begins in order to recover man and bring him back to a normal relation with God. It is the first step to perfection, to being inhabited by the Holy Spirit once again, like in the beginning. This first step is an ideological reflection of the people's hearts of that time, just as the laws of Moses are a reflection of people's feeble spiritual powers of his time, and the laws of Jesus Christ reflect a fully grown spiritual age.

There are several stages of this process that defines man's relation with the animals, with his food, his thoughts on certain things, etc. We see this process more clearly explained by Jesus in the Gospel of Mark:

"He answered them, "What did Moses command you?" They said, "Moses allowed a man to write a certificate of divorce and to send her away." And Jesus

*said to them, "**Because of your hardness of heart he wrote you this commandment**." Mark, 10, 3-5*

So Jesus shows clearly to anyone who pays attention the process through which the Lord gives temporary orders to the patient, depending on what his illness needs. The Lord gives temporary and eternal orders. The episode of Abraham who is ordered to kill his own son and is stopped by God on the verge of doing it is an example of a temporary order, given only to teach Abraham, for his spiritual evolution. Although the commandments given in the Leviticus, through Moses, forbid man to eat all kinds of "unclean" animals, even to touch them on the Sabbath day and settle many such rules, one more rigid than the other, Jesus Christ gives more freedom with his laws, addressed this time to spiritual men and not to spiritual children, as was the case with the laws given through the mouth of Moses:

"It is not what goes into the mouth that defiles a person, but what comes out of the mouth; this defiles a person ... Do you not see that whatever goes into the mouth passes into the stomach and is expelled? But what comes out of the mouth proceeds from the heart, and this defiles a person" Matthew 15, 11-17

What about the unclean animals which man was forbidden to eat? The answer is found in the Acts of the

Apostles, where this is said to the Apostle Peter through godly vision:

"What God has made clean, do not call common."
Acts 11:9

Apparently, they were unclean only if God forbade man to eat them. They were unclean because, by eating them, man disobeyed the Lord and thus lost his communion with the Holy Spirit. On the other hand, God gives laws to teach man obedience and he can thus receive the other gifts of the Holy Spirit, which only the man who has acquired a complex understanding through humble obedience can receive and use. It is for these gifts from the Holy Spirit and for the communion with the Holy Spirit that the Lord gives all kinds of laws, according to man's needs to control his heart. They are nothing more but spiritual crutches.

The last level of laws is the one that the Apostle Paul talks about, namely a level where there are no more crutches, because the communion with the Holy Spirit is complete and through Him, man sees all the enemy's traps and can only fall in them by his own will, not by being tricked:

"*All things are lawful for me, but not all things are helpful. All things are lawful for me, but I will not be enslaved by anything.*" 1 Corinthians 6, 12

This is the first level where one can say they leave the childish life and enter the manly life, according to the Apostle Paul's words, which come from the Holy Spirit:

"*When I was a child, I talked like a child, I thought like a child, I reasoned like a child. When I became a man, I put the ways of childhood behind me. For now we see only a reflection as in a mirror; then we shall see face to face. Now I know in part; then I shall know fully, even as I am fully known.*" 1 Corinthians 13, 12

Question 11:

"9:4 But you shall not eat flesh with its life, that is, its blood. And for your lifeblood I will require a reckoning: from every beast I will require it and from man. From his fellow man I will require a reckoning for the life of man. Whoever sheds the blood of man, by man shall his blood be shed, for God made man in his own image."

So does this mean that meat should be well cooked and not have blood in it?

The reason why God forbade eating blood is a paradoxical one. Man is allowed to kill the animal and eat it, hit it in the head, cut its throat, bite away its flesh, in other words he can destroy it, but not allowed to drink the animal blood while you do all the things shown above. God's temporary laws are paradoxical, but they teach us about the details and relations of the entire Creation, both material and spiritual:

"Any Israelite or any foreigner residing among you who hunts any animal or bird that may be eaten must drain out the blood and cover it with earth, because the life of every creature is its blood.

*That is why I have said to the Israelites, **"You must not eat the blood of any creature, because the life of every creature is its blood; anyone who eats it must be cut off.**"* Leviticus 17, 13-14

Let's look again to the example of Abraham, who knew how Cain had been punished for the sin of killing and was aware of God's eternal will with regard to taking another man's life. But when God tells him to kill a man, who happens to be Abraham's own son, he does not question this temporary law.

What pattern do we notice here? It's a cat-and-mouse game in which we find out that the laws of the Lord belong to the Lord only. He can give them and take them back when and as He pleases. He can change their priority and manufacture them with any parameters He likes. The entire order of the world was decided by the Lord from the beginning. And He is the one who can change it a thousand ways and a thousand times. We see, for example, in the episode when God wishes to destroy the chosen people, but does not, due to the pleading of Moses in Exodus chapter 32. In other words, the Lord was about to alter the plan for man's redemption and to apply major changes to it. We know this because we cannot accuse God of using the little trick called reverse psychology on Moses. We see also in

Numbers 20 that Moses pleaded for the water requested forcefully by his people. In fact, Moses is punished not to enter Canaan because of his many pleadings, which shows us how much determined was God to change the plan regarding the people He delivered from Egypt.

The pattern of this law about eating blood teaches us that the Lord uses the laws to teach us obedience. He teaches us that the only parameter that should not change in our relation with Him is our obedience to Him. Drawing conclusions based on our knowledge of God's laws is bound to fail because the human subject or the non-human subject, the angels, who does this, claims omniscience and omnipotence powers, which he does not have and will never have.

How should man's relation to God develop? Through humble obedience, man will be able to understand what God reveals to him at one point or another in the history of man's soul.

There are two ways for knowing God: the **cataphatic** way and the **apophatic** way.

The Cataphatic Way consists in **what we know** about the Lord, knowing the Lord through Laws, be they rational (ideas), or physical (the Univers).

The Apophatic Way consists of **what we don't know** about the Lord, knowing the Lord through what He shows us otherwise than through Laws, i.e. through Grace.

God wants us to know His laws, but he wants even more, that we know Him as much as we could. Whoever wishes to know only the divine laws and not the Lord Himself does that for a personal agenda and so he wishes to usurp the Lord's position. Such a person is interested in power through advanced and sufficient knowledge of the laws, in order to manipulate them for a rebel purpose. Whoever wishes to know the Lord is also indirectly interested in the Lord's Laws. This is the rightful way of knowing the Lord, as showed in the Psalms:

"As a deer pants for flowing streams, so pants my soul for you, O God." Psalm 42, The wish to know the Lord.

"Send out your light and your truth; let them lead me; let them bring me to your holy hill and to your dwelling!" Psalm 43, Using the Grace (the Light) and the Laws (the Truth) to get to the Lord.

This is where the relation between the Grace and the Laws is obvious. One can understand or see the

Laws, which are God's Truth, only by Grace, which is God's Light. And man needs both to reach God. The act of faith happens when we obey the Laws even before the Grace explains them to us, only out of the wish to know the Lord and to obey Him. Faith means we listen because **we want to start the relationship with the Lord**, not because we are compelled to listen by the data we receive, data that may include information about Heaven or Hell.

Abraham understood by Grace the order of killing his son. And we understand now by Grace that we are not allowed to eat blood, as God uses this liquid/material in his plan to deify us, through the sacrament of communion (the Eucharist) established by Jesus Christ. Man is allowed to drink only the blood of our Saviour, so that he may commune with Him and be deified as we can clearly see it written in Mathew chapter 26:

"Then he took a cup, and when he had given thanks, he gave it to them, saying, "Drink from it, all of you. This is my blood of the covenant, which is poured out for many for the forgiveness of sins. I tell you, I will not drink from this fruit of the vine from now on until that day when I drink it new with you in my Father's kingdom." Mathew 26, 27-29

This idea is detailed in John chapter 6:

> "Your ancestors ate the manna in the wilderness, yet they died. But here is the bread that comes down from heaven, which anyone may eat and not die. I am the living bread that came down from heaven. Whoever eats this bread will live forever. This bread is my flesh, which I will give for the life of the world."
>
> Then the Jews began to argue sharply among themselves, "How can this man give us his flesh to eat?"
>
> Jesus said to them, "Very truly I tell you, **unless you eat the flesh of the Son of Man and drink his blood, you have no life in you**. Whoever eats my flesh and drinks my blood has eternal life, and I will raise them up at the last day.
>
> For my flesh is real food and my blood is real drink. Whoever eats my flesh and drinks my blood remains in me, and I in them. Just as the living Father sent me and I live because of the Father, so the one who feeds on me will live because of me. This is the bread that came down from heaven. Your ancestors ate manna and died, but whoever feeds on this bread will live forever." He said this while teaching in the synagogue in Capernaum." John 6, 49-59

The blood is not the only liquid of Man which is given spiritual importance by God.

The seed is another important liquid, which is to be particularly respected as giver of life and identity, able even to make us inherit both the sins and the blessings of our parents and great-great-grandparents:

*"You shall not bow down to them or worship them; for I, the L*ORD *your God, am a jealous God,* **punishing the children for the sin of the parents** *to the* **third and fourth generation** *of those who hate me, but* **showing love to a thousand generations of those who love me and keep my commandments."**
Exodus 20, 5-6

The hair, the vow of the Nazirite, who were Old Testament saints of God, is also related to man's identity.

*"During the entire period of their Nazirite vow, no razor may be used on their head. They must be holy until the period of their dedication to the L*ORD *is over; they must let their hair grow long."* Number 6, 5

We can see that everything related to man's body is treated differently from the body of the other beings;

thus, man's body is considered holy. All of these come from the mystery of man being made in the Image of God.

In fact, the entire human body and soul is deemed the temple of the Lord, as called in the books of the New Testament many times:

*"Do you not know that you are God's temple and that God's Spirit dwells in you? If anyone destroys God's temple, God will destroy him. For **God's temple is holy**, and **you are that temple.**"* 1 Corinthians 3, 16-17

Question 12:

What does it mean that *"God created man in His own image"*?

God created man in His own image, but He didn't stop there. He took a human body when the Word became a man called Jesus and now He sits in Heaven, the holiest place, with this human image, this body he turned from mortal and ephemeral into immortal and eternal. He promised us, too, that we would keep our bodies after our resurrection in the last day and that He would make them immortal and eternal as well.

My question is: what is the purpose of this mystery of God? Why did God, who could create whatever He wanted, fight the devil in whatever form He wanted, defend His creation in whatever form He chose, as everything is possible for God, so why did He want so much to get a human image?

What is the most hidden and profound relation between the Lord and His decision of giving man His image and to take, in His turn, a human image for eternity?

We know that God made us only in His own *image*, and although his intention is for us to be in His *likeness*, he let that part of the job for us. As it is written in the Genesis 1, 26-27 *"Let Us make man in Our image, according to Our likeness" ... "So God created mankind in his own image"*, we can clearly see that God intention is for us to finish the last part and to become transformed more into His likeness.

For that to happened God decided to test our freewill and this test came in the Garden of Eden through a simple Command, through a simple temporary boundary that He imposed. What happened next is that man needed to learn the hard way. So God proceeded to recuperate man form his error, first by making clothes for him and then by involving him deeply in his own healing process when he put him to work for a living and make him appreciate each aspect of the nature that God created for man and of his own life. This hard lesson was chosen instead of a soft lesson because soft lessons do not teach to the extent a hard lesson does, they are not equal in their outcome as we can clearly see in the example of the soft lesson that Satan received. The "morning star" angel was kept as an angel even after his intentions were made clear and could even approach God from time to time. He is still receiving this soft lesson because at any time he chooses Satan can turn to God and ask for forgiveness which **he knows** that he will receive it if only he will turn to God.

However this hard lesson is now, after Christ did everything he needed to do to save us, it is totally dependent of man's freewill and can cease at a moment notice if man will only "open his eyes to the Sun". Since man keeps his eyes closed or partially closed on his own volition, the hard lesson continues by default. This lesson is composed from many parts, some of which will be explained here:

1. The need to be (in that order) merciful, tolerant, than civil, empathic and finally loving towards all the beings around you, be they human beings or not.
2. The need to be grateful for all of God's gifts, starting with the material gifts and ending with the spiritual ones: each and every little gift should receive its own profound reconnaissance and thanks.
3. The need to sort your thoughts out on what exactly you want from God. This should be simple as God's gifts are not to be desire without the presence of God, since all God's gifts are not enough to keep us satisfied. The conclusion is that we should concentrate all our attention and thoughts on God Himself.
4. The need to overcome our selfishness and evil through our obedience to God's Commands. That

is the hard one and we might need help on that task from our brothers and especially from God. The good news is that at least God is there for us, helping us with all His Might.

The answer to the question of "**Why** God wanted to make us in his image and likeness?" remains a mystery until the Holy Spirit will reveal it to us at the time and to the extent decided by Him. Whatever we may read and learn on this subject, this question will remain in part a mystery to us because it cannot be fully grasped by human intelligence since this creation act is a decision coming from the Essence of the Lord, which will always stay inaccessible to us. The difference between a mystery of God and an enigma is that the enigma, once become known, stop being an enigma. The mystery of God remains a mystery even after it becomes known by a creature, as it comes from the Essence of the Lord and can only be fully known by the Lord, who is the only one who has full access to His Essence.

The mystery of the relation between the Lord's image and likeness and the human image is also directly related to the Sacrament of the Eucharist, the communion of man with holiness by means of the Lord's body and blood. Another aspect is that the Lord calls the body "the temple of the Lord", in other words, the place where He wishes to live. Our journey in finding out "Who we really are?" and "Why are we who we are?" will stretch beyond our earthly life, beyond our temporary death and even beyond our resurrection into our eternal life in God's Heaven.

Question 13:

CHAPTER 9

"18. The sons of Noah who went forth from the ark were Shem, Ham, and Japheth.
19. These three were the sons of Noah, and from these the people of the whole earth were dispersed.
20. Noah began to be a man of the soil, and he planted a vineyard.
21. He drank of the wine and became drunk and lay uncovered in his tent.
22. And Ham, the father of Canaan, saw the nakedness of his father and told his two brothers outside.
23. Then Shem and Japheth took a garment, laid it on both their shoulders, and walked backward and covered the nakedness of their father. Their faces were turned backward, and they did not see their father's nakedness..
24. When Noah awoke from his wine and knew what his youngest son had done to him,
25. He said: "Cursed be Canaan; a servant of servants shall he be to his brothers."
26. He also said: "Blessed be the LORD, the God of Shem; and let Canaan be his servant!

27. May God enlarge Japheth, and let him dwell in the tents of Shem and let Canaan be his servant."

Why did Noah curse Canaan instead of Ham? Or, if the children must suffer because of their parent's sins, why didn't Noah curse Ham, as well?

Did he bless Japheth, too, but less than Shem? What kind of blessing is for Japheth to live in Shem's tents?

The curse was cast on the child, who suffered for his father's sin. There was no need for his father to be cursed, as he fell from Grace the moment he committed the sin. We can't expect the divine justice to apply only to the child, while the father is well off, enjoying the Holy Spirit. So, Ham's punishment is the fall from Grace and everything that comes with it. Canaan's punishment is having Ham as a father, as he is the seed and blood of Ham and, thus, he inherits all of Ham's virtues and sins, blessing and curses from God.

We all carry Adam's sin with us, from birth, a sin which is cleaned by baptism, as we are Adam's seed. Jesus as God's Word precedes Adam and so He is not coming from the first Man. That is why He is sinless from the very beginning. God-Jesus took upon Him the burden of Adam's sin without being guilty of this sin: Disobedience from Father. Adam's sin was his disobedience started in the Garden of Eden, but Jesus repaired this sin by obedience to the Lord throughout His life and in His death. A good example in this respect is the cup episode on the Mount of Olives, where God's Will was deemed perfect by the Son, despite the fact that Father was asking his Son to pay for Man's Sin, in order to give Man one last chance and a way of coming back to the Father. The Lord's curse is related to the human morphology, "the image of man", which includes both man's body and soul, and the way in which these operate in the sinner and his heirs, all of us being the children of this fistful of earth named Adam and from the same breath of life that was given to him.

Thus, the Death that comes from Adam's disobedience is transmitted to all of Adam's heirs through the seed perpetuated by men in their endeavours with women, just like the eternal life of Jesus Christ's obedience enters all those who welcome Him in their souls by faith and in their bodies by the Holy Communion.

Shem was Noah's first born, as he is the first on the list of Noah's sons described in Chapter 6 and in Chapter

10, verse 21. So, as ruled by God, he received the blessing to become patriarch after his father's death. Japheth is blessed to live in Shem's grace. To live in someone's tents means to share the holiness and God's gifts for that house. In less symbolic words, it means to be one of the saints of the Lord, one of the sons of the God, receiving the same blessing from God as Shem.

Although Ham had been one of the sons of God, he fell from that position, which is proven by the fact that Canaan's sons ended all as servants of Israel, a descendant of Shem, through his son, Arfaxad:

"Canaan fathered Sidon his firstborn and Heth, and the Jebusites, the Amorites, the Girgashites, the Hivites, the Arkites, the Sinites, the Arvadites, the Zemarites, and the Hamathites. Afterward the clans of the Canaanites dispersed." Genesis 10, 15-18

Ham's fall from among the sons of God is also obvious through Ham's other sons: from Mizraim and his son, Casluhim there come the Philistines that fought the Israelites.

All the "sons of men" served other gods, while the "sons of God" served only the Living God.

To these "sons of men", God opposes the "sons of God" in the war for the conquest of Canaan showed in the Book of Joshua of Navi:

"Here is how you shall know that the living God is among you and that he will without fail drive out from before you the Canaanites, the Hittites, the Hivites, the Perizzites, the Girgashites, the Amorites, and the Jebusites." Joshua Navi 3, 10

The only justification of the war for Canaan was to show that the blessings given to Shem were fulfilled for the sons of God, so **for Shem's children**, and that the curse cast on the "sons of men", the heirs of Ham and Canaan, became true.

Japheth as son of God will have his blessing fulfilled when he multiplied in so many tribes that took so much land and later by living in Shem's spiritual tent or temple, which is the Word of God, Jesus Christ. We see that Jesus is establishing Himself as the Spiritual and Material Temple of God here:

The Material Temple: *"Jesus answered and said to them, "Destroy this temple, and in three days I will raise it up."* John 2, 19

The Spiritual Temple: *"But the hour is coming, and now is, when the true worshipers will worship the Father in spirit and truth; for the Father is seeking such to worship Him. God is Spirit, and those who worship Him must worship in spirit and truth."* John 4, 23-24

"Jesus said to him, "I am the way, the truth, and the life. No one comes to the Father except through Me." John 14, 6

Now we know that when the Second temple existed only Jews could approach and make sacrifices there as atonement for their sins. But after Jesus Christ became the Third and last Temple of God, the Temple of God was opened to all people and Japheth children eagerly received their blessings trough "Shem's tents", the Apostles, that were all Jews and all Japheth tribes, first the ones in Europe and than from other places, started to receive the true God through the works of the Holy Spirit. Since Ham's children already received their punishments trough Canaan War, they too were included in God's blessing towards all men:

"Therefore I make known to you that no one speaking by the Spirit of God says, "Jesus is accursed"; and no one can say, "Jesus is Lord," except by the Holy Spirit." 1 Corinthians 12, 3

Naturally, in the Holy Scriptures we see many such prophecies coming true and completing each other, all being part of the Great Divine Plan of God. All the prophecies teach the laws of the Lord, and the blessings and curses are the "sentences" by which these laws are sometimes transmitted to us. The laws are made to get us as close as possible to the condition of son of God, of pure vessel of the Holy Spirit.

Laws are made so that we may know Grace. Grace makes us sons of God, as by Grace we know the Messiah, the Son of God, Jesus Christ, who is the Truth.

"He was in the world, and the world was made through Him, and the world did not know Him. He came to His own, and His own did not receive Him. But as many as received Him, to them He gave the right to become children of God, to those who believe in His name: who were born, not of blood, nor of the will of the flesh, nor of the will of man, but of God." John 1, 10-13

"And you will know the truth and the truth will set you free" John 8, 32

PART III

"The Beginning of Wisdom"

Proverbs 9,10

Fear of the Lord and of His Mercy

"The fear of the Lord is the beginning of wisdom." Psalm 9, 10

Everything that comes from man is imperfect, subject to error, unworthy of being taken into consideration. Man must be silent within and listen. An attentive man is silent and is listening. In order to be consonant with Holiness, man must let God speak through him, his contribution consisting in listening to the message transmitted through him, for him and for the others.

Man must be glad and sad, at the same time. He should be glad, because God forgives his mistakes. He should be sad, because man keeps making mistakes. Man is in a perpetual state of error, with the constant hope for perfection. He must let himself be imbued by God and keep his mind silent, putting an end to the storm of thoughts and the inner dialogue that his relation with God causes within his soul.

Man should constantly hope for God's Mercy, but without abuse and neglect. God's Mercy is a gift, like the other divine gifts in man's life. It is not a right, but a **holy gift**.

God's Mercy is the Lord's **holiness** put in practice. Visible holiness is: having children, the air we breathe, our health, the coherent thinking process we depend on so much. Therefore, we must get closer to this Mercy, Grace, Holiness, only when we've removed our "shoes" to show respect and reverence, as Moses was rightfully asked to do before the burning bush.

On the Immortality of Man

Man has the duty to accept and endure the Lord's creation as meant for him to endure every day. He must not oppose what is given daily unless he is inspired by God to do so or receives a clear revelation from God that he must oppose, if the lesson consists in this very act: opposition because of contradiction to God's Laws. As long as man does not succeed in perfectly obeying his Lord, he is decayed from the responsible condition of holy creature, becomes irresponsible and an offense both to himself, as a rebel against his own meaning and nature, and to his Creator, as a rebel against His laws.

After all, man faces many times the road to survival or to death. This choice is given to test man's obedience to the commands of his Creator, sometimes receiving "trial by fire" on many subjects. Man needs to obey God's Laws and not to oppose his ordeal within reason, as Jonah wrongly did, even if this means his physical dissolution. Therefore, man must obey the

Lord even with the price of his life, because the lesson is about just that. Man may oppose other people provided they violate the laws and moral values given by God, but man's opposition must under no circumstances result in destructively hurting or destroying the others. He must take into account that "the enemy" before him is his twin brother.

Man is immortal and, due to this reality, the equation of his survival is solved, even beyond temporal boundaries of the Universe. All man has to do is to be faithful to this gift, Immortality, given to him by God.

Immortality is a divine gift that solves the problem of man's survival on earth and of all the decisions arising from this dilemma.

Question: What should I oppose the ordeal given to me so that I may survive? Answer: Nothing. Man does not **need** to survive physically. Man already is and will always be immortal.

The next question, of course, is: what kind of immortality do you want to have?

The Hero, the Saint, the Martyr and Their Failed Version, the Genius

The genius is the maximum sum of man's rational and affective capabilities, but without an active moral component.

It is the moral component that gives eternal value and, as such, the only real value, to all human actions. The moral component comes directly from the divine laws, from the authority of God and **cannot be overruled by any other purpose**. Thus, the divine morals also define the means to use for reaching the purpose of the divine laws.

The Hero, the Saint and the Martyr access all the stairs of human accomplishment, due to their momentary conduct, thus fulfilling the complete Human Model. Among these three categories of people, nevertheless, only the Saint lives according to the divine morals beyond the present moment, for eternity. The other two categories may succumb, in extreme circumstances, back to the decayed man's condition. This is why the condition of heroism and martyrdom depends exclusively on God's mercy, expressed by circumstances that are favourable to heroic or martyr-like deeds, the condition of holiness being a sustained effort of both divinity and humans.

The Saint is the only human category that can be a Hero and a Martyr at the same time, because he lives consciously in God's kingdom on earth, while the other two categories only catch a glimpse at it at the time of the heroic act or of their martyrdom. The Saint, nevertheless, cannot declare himself a martyr, not even when he is martyred, as he loves his executioners too much to judge them or to hand them to God's justice. So he forgives them and has enough force to tell his executioners that he forgives them, thus even causing a few comical moments, as the executioners become fiercely angry faced with the saint's "insensitiveness" to the torment they apply to him. The Saint even intervenes for his oppressors before God who, in His turn, may make a miracle and absolve the executioners on the spot, changing their hearts by momentarily imbuing them with Holy Spirit, with understanding and high spiritual sight, as in the case of Saul and his men, when they were trying to persecute David (1 Kings, 19, 24).

The Saint will not dare to become a Hero for two reasons: he does not want to expose himself to vain glory and he cannot hate any creature of the Lord, however evil they are or may be, because he loves all creation, with all his heart. He will only reprimand the evil creatures, yet leaving them all the freedom to act, leaving their will intact, just like God who, most of the time, decides to allow the freewill to manifest itself, even if it takes horrible forms. The Saint will not judge his executioners also out of love for the witnesses of his martyrdom, so that he may be a moral educational example for them, a living example of catechisation.

The Hero is the expression of God's justice on earth, feeling in each breath the purity of God's word on the universal order, as expressed by the moral hierarchy of the created world:
- God;
- The angelic powers;
- The Saint, the complete man, made holy by God;
- The wise man, the incomplete, but spiritually improved man; very probable a hero or a martyr;

- The common man, obedient to the divine morals, but burdened with worries; possibly a hero or a martyr, with God's mercy;

- The common man who does not obey the divine morals out of selfishness; possibly, in very special conditions to become an ad-hoc hero or martyr, with God's mercy;

- The evil man, totally surrendered to evil; the opposite of the hero;

- The devilish powers.

This moral hierarchy is a real state of fact and results in the universal order, the scale we refer to in order to see where we stand at a given moment in time. This moral order is given by the sum of the virtues and vices, in all their forms and at all their levels, similar to a vertical ladder we climb up or down. This ladder should be used wisely, as sometimes, climbing it up due to a virtue could be a trap set by the enemy; if it is not use wisely even a virtue can lead to a vice.

Thus, when the Hero sees that the hierarchy and the order are disturbed by the actions of an evil party, for example, an attack against the moral innocence of a victim or of a mass of victims, he wishes to restore the moral order by his actions, being different from the Saint by the fact that he is not spiritually powerful enough to wait and let God restore this order when He thinks fit. The Hero will take a stand, inspired by God, and will give that moment divine inspiration by visibly restoring, even if only for the moment, the true moral order. The Hero may thus become a Martyr, and the Martyr who chose to be a martyr is and will always be a Hero.

Even if the Hero lacks the depth of the Saint's faith, he is no less pleasing to God, as God tries to bring man at his highest level of spiritual feeling and, if this is the Hero's level, then it is best for him to remain forever at this level trough his deeds and to turn from a common man into a Hero, than to fall back in the cowardice specific to the common man. Another positive effect is that, once a Hero, free from fear and, so, from cowardice, the common man finds it easier to take a step towards one form or another of martyrdom and, so, become a Martyr and be absolved through his sacrifice.

Martyrdom is heroism led to its final extreme conclusion: rather than witnessing the destruction of the moral order by the evil forces and undertake a fearful survival in this new, hideous, evil "order", the Hero prefers to leave this desecrated earth by the odious hands of the sinners who will kill him, and enter the moral order ensured by life after death. Life in the spiritual world is an exclusively divine field, without any right to question who holds the keys of this land and who makes order in there. It is a land under the total and visible control of God.

The difference between life on earth and life in the spiritual world is that, according to God's plan, this material world, the material creation is shared, in terms of power, with the evil forces, in order to sift the wheat from the chaff and, thus, to enforce the eternal divine justice, to see who deserves to sit next to God and who chooses to stay afar from him, in the place of eternal pain, where the evil ones will be cut off from God. Consequently, the evil forces are left to do their job the best they can here on earth, to change, even if illusively, the moral order of the world, denying reality, God, and His gifts given to the creatures beneath Him.

All of these three moral categories: the Saint, the Martyr and the Hero submit their rational and affective capabilities to the moral component, as they know that all the gifts come from God and He alone deserves the glory. Therefore, the Saints, the Martyrs and the Heroes will not praise their many rational or affective qualities, but will praise the Lord for giving them these qualities and the wisdom to use them right.

The Genius is an exception to the human categories above, as he is different from the common man due to all of his rational and affective gifts with which he was endowed by God. Since these gifts do not obey his soul weakened by the sin, they end up working against him in a chaotic manner, either by attracting praises he does not deserve and which are illusory (the sin of fake glory), leading even to madness (denial of God), or by despair, because he cannot properly manage these gifts so as to bring joy and spiritual satisfaction upon himself and others. This means that the Genius, not being morally perfect, cannot share his gifts in a morally correct way, giving God what belongs to Him, i.e. glory and thanks for his gifts.

Genius is not a positive moral category, and a genial man does not surpass, morally speaking, the common man, who is morally corrupted, as many times, the gifts he received from God are not used for his own spiritual evolution or others, but for his own glory. Thus, the use of such gifts becomes an unjust and ungrateful deed in terms of the moral order of the world.

Although the Genius is adulated and praised by common, unwise men, who think this is the maximum level they can reach, this reasoning must be proven false and based on false assumptions, as man's spiritual evolution is accomplished by using the God's gifts, to be able to reach new moral levels, and not for new rational or affective levels.

The rational and affective powers were created and subordinated to the spirit's moral powers because, without a decision-maker (the Holy Spirit who advises man's spirit) and rules (the divine laws), these numerous and varied spiritual gifts may be an occasion for giving in to vices and sins, for climbing down the moral ladder, instead of up.

The Genius is a moral failure also because he accepts men's praise without fully denying it, without trying to explain to his fellow men that his gifts are just that: gifts from God and not his own achievements.

Due to his gifts, the Genius often has easier access to all the human categories of the Moral Hierarchy, being able to become first a spiritually improved man, then a wise man, then a Saint, including the Martyr and the Hero. But, most times, we see the Genius intoxicated with vain glory and separated from God, who endowed him with so many gifts. He falls among the incapable, spiritually weak men and remains a pathetic human being, who does not succeed in rising to the greatness and beauty of the Complete Man, the Saint.

The modern ideology, which is far from the Christian faith, praises the Genius in order to deceive us and to alienate us from the ideals of the morally accomplished man, by displaying the material or falsely spiritual benefits of a Genius, the first being vain glory. The greatest fear of this ideology is a direct confrontation between the Saint and the Genius, the two ideals, a heavenly one and a devilish one. Such a confrontation that uses all the arguments of the true, real world, of God's order, as He designed it, shows us that the Genius is at the bottom of the human success ladder and that, in fact, he is not different than many others that succumbed to the temptation of vain.

Thus, although full of gifts, but arrogant as Satan, the Genius will lose the fight with the simple, poor Saint, because, in terms of property over the gifts, they are all God's exclusive property and, as such, talents lent by Him, for a price (see *"parable of the talents"* Mathew 25, 14-30, Luke 19, 11-27).

God uses both the abundance and the lack of gifts to test man. He wants to see how Man uses them and, so, who becomes a Saint, a complete man and who doesn't.

He gives these talents with an expensive interest, which is man's eternal life itself.

Confrontation between Two Human Ideals: the Saint and the Genius

As a human ideal, the Saint is the sum of the dreams and hopes of fallen Adam.

A human being endowed with gifts, but not with wisdom, Adam fell, despite his intelligence and insight. Adam was profound and complex, strong and fearless, intelligent and efficient, yet not completely united with God, not yet a spiritual son of the Lord, but merely a son in flesh and bones. Although God asked Adam to name the animals and, thus, to complete His creation, once Adam ate from the Tree of Knowledge and fell from Eden, God no longer trusted that he had the spiritual power to refrain from eating from the Tree of Life, as well.

Therefore, we see that even when Adam was in the Garden of Eden, far from all the suffering, he was not wise in all spiritual aspects. After his fall, Adam must have wondered all his life what his mistake had been and how he could have avoided giving in to temptation. So he dreamt all his life to the ideal of the Saint, who not only obeys the Lord, but is a close friend to God and loves God more than His gifts.

Although the Saint does not have all the gifts at any given time, he has access to these gifts, either by the will of God, as God wishes to ennoble him with gifts for his obedience, or by the will of the Saint, who sometimes wishes for gifts so he can successfully accomplish his mission of restoring man (all the fallen men) to his initial condition, when he knew no suffering, with some extra wisdom so that he may never fall again.

The saints may ask for **natural gifts**, such as intelligence, profound understanding and the gift of speaking, of easy and efficient communication. An example in this respect is Saint Spyridon, a simple shepherd in the Isle of Cyprus, who, at the First Synod of Nicaea, explained the Gospel so powerfully to a heretic philosopher who came on behalf of Arius that the philosopher kept silent, as if he had nothing more to say. The philosopher could not speak against the saint, which irradiated a godly rational and mystic power. A renowned man in the cultural environment of that time, the philosopher was one of the heretics of Arius, who knew many languages and could provide many biblical or scientific arguments. He was such a scholar that he dared confront the great theologian of that time, Saint Athanasius the Great (of Alexandria), to whom he said: "Give me a text of the Gospel and I'll give you 10,000". It is this philosopher that the heretics of Arius bragged about and considered as their champion, and with whom they hoped to destroy the orthodox belief according to which the Saviour had a divine nature, at the Great Ecumenical Synod where, among others, it was decided on the correct understanding of the Holy Trinity.

The saints may even ask for **supernatural gifts**, as we can see at the same First Ecumenical Synod at Nicaea. Thus, Saint Spyridon was given the gift of splitting a brick in the three elements it was made of: fire, water and earth, in his hand, at room temperature. The godly power shown through this miracle was enough to frighten all those present, who did not share the faith of the orthodox priests and who tried to oppose them with all kinds of arguments. The saint's demonstration, which was both natural, through words and supernatural, through a miracle, solved the Holy Trinity subject for ever.

The saints also request gifts for others, as when Saint Ephrem the Syrian wished to speak to Saint Basil the Great, but could not speak Greek; so Saint Basil the Great asked the Lord to make Saint Ephrem able to speak and understand Greek, just for a little while. God changed Saint Ephrem's language so there were no communication barriers between the two great saints.

The saints **may ask for and have** all the gifts of the complete man, who is not limited by the barriers imposed on the sinful men by God, as God Himself promised:

"And I tell you, ask, and it will be given to you;"
"If you then, who are evil, know how to give good gifts to your children, how much more will the heavenly Father give the Holy Spirit to those who ask Him!" Luke 11, 9-13

We see in the Lord's words above that the gift comes through the Holy Spirit, as Grace, an exclusively godly energy. This is why the common sinners may ask for Grace through their prayers, each according to their needs; so, they pray for understanding, for advice, even for supernatural healing, if this is their need. God's only condition is that the gift man asks for be a good gift in the context it is asked for. If God does not grant it, then a lesson must be learned.

The saints may be as fast as the wind, as smart as the angels, as strong as the mythic heroes from the ancient human myths. They can turn inanimate objects into animate objects and vice-versa, depending on the spiritual and material needs of the people they try to help, as it is described in the numerous cases where the saints perform miracles for the poor of the world, by making gold or other precious metals.

The saints are at all times aware that God's gifts are theirs to use, but not to possess; they are not their property. But they use such gifts freely and as needed.

The saints are masters at correctly using the gifts, as they do not wish to achieve vain glory through them. On the contrary, they enjoy not so much the gift itself, but its effect of restoring man to his initial condition.

The situation is different for the **Genius**, an ideal and champion for modern ideology, which is broken away from God. The genius can have one or several gifts, but he cannot have all of them at the same time or sequentially. While the Saints possess all the natural and, especially, the supernatural gifts, geniuses are limited to a small number of gifts and they can never have supernatural gifts.

The Genius's understanding of his gift can be advanced, but it can also be insufficient, in which case this gift will cause much suffering to the Genius. Even when he understands his gift, the Genius sometimes finds it very difficult to benevolently share it with the world and starts using it incorrectly. This means he does not use it for the benefit of the common man, but shows off, to gain a certain status and wealth rather than to help people.

There have been cases of geniuses who rightfully gave their gift to their less endowed fellow men of the time, but once they became pious, they gave up the status of Genius or never accepted it as such. Such an example is the composer Johann Sebastian Bach, who was endowed with a great gift for understanding music, as well as for transmitting spiritual feelings through this artistic means. Although a musical genius and even one of the main pillars of the cult music over the past 400 years, Bach did not try to rise to a better status than the one useful for his work as a composer, trying to acquire not human power, but power over his gift, creative power, to rejoice his fellow men.

Nevertheless, other geniuses did not manage to have such a disciplined and controlled conduct as Bach and, because of their gift, they decayed and lost not only their mind, but also their spirit, their chance to reach human perfection.

The mistake of the Genius does not consist only in how he uses this gift or how he shares it with his fellow men. The fatal mistake of the Genius is that he does not see the gift as a test given to him by God to sieve through the sins of his soul and sort the material, but mostly, the spiritual benefits of this gift. Apparently, geniuses do not understand that their gift is a treasure that God lays upon them, to watch them use it for the small and the poor in this world (Matthew, 18:10), including himself. The deeper the Genius understands the heart of the Lord, the better he will manage his gift for God's creation.

The gift given to the Genius is the Lord's spiritual richness pouring out on the world through a human channel. But in the process of using the gift and sharing it with the world, this channel (the Genius) can lose himself, being left in the end with no benefit in the eternal life after the life on earth. Sometimes, the Genius ends up losing his soul precisely through the gift that was an extraordinary mercy and honour given to him by God.

God's gift will definitely save others, as any gift of God is a power that lifts the soul. But the one who is most exposed to the danger of losing himself through this gift is the one who handles and serves the gift: the Genius.

The men of modern ideology have always seen the Genius as the ideal they aspire to, to the detriment of the ideal given by God to humanity: the Saint. God certifies the Saint through miracles and so, the Genius must bow his spirit to the power of God, which is visible through the Saints. Nevertheless, the men of modern ideology have ignored the Saint and praised the Genius because, if they can prove that the Genius is more powerful than the Saint, as ideal, then, in their minds that ignore where the gifts come from, they no longer need God.

How nicely God shows us where the gifts of **intelligence and knowledge** - which are mundane, lay gifts - come from:

"The LORD said to Moses, "See, I have called by name Bezalel, the son of Uri, son of Hur, of the tribe of Judah, and I have filled him with the Spirit of God,

with ability and intelligence, with knowledge and all craftsmanship, to devise artistic designs, to work in gold, silver, and bronze." Exodus 31, 1-4

People who are ignorant of God and rebel against Him, in their blindness, obstinately refuse to understand that the gift, even the gift of a Genius, is the very channel of communication between their souls and … God. The gift is to be respected, but God is to be respected before the gift, knowing and adoring Him being the purpose and end of the gift.

⚘ ⑲ ⚘

Asceticism and Fulfillment
About the end of the life of Abba Sisoes the Great

Somewhere into the depths of the Sketis desert, a place far away from any villages and even farther from the cities, there lived a man of God, a monk named Sisoes, who worked for his redemption through ascetic life.

The mystical thoughts kept him company and guided him in the life path of his choice. Theology was his life, but he did not specifically or intentionally meditate upon that, for he found it more important to reach the redemption of sins through any simple means he could use. Many went to see him and ask him about theological or ascetic ideas and he tried to tell them what he knew, nevertheless showing them that the most important thing was not the one they were asking about, but being simple and placing themselves "below any creature", in order to be securely humble.

His humble life was full of miraculous events: sometimes he brought the dead back to life by mistake, some other times he chased the demons away by simply saying a word to God. The miracles happened naturally and unwillingly and he asked his close ones to spare him the fake glory by talking about his miracles and their meaning only after his death.

After Abba Anthony the Great passed to his heavenly reward, the hermit Sisoes arrived at the great saint's cave and turned it into his new dwelling, with a simple word of humility: "Thus, in the lion's cave, a fox nestled". Later on, when asked by a brother why he had moved in Great Anthony's cave, he answered that he wanted to stay for a little while in such a quiet cave and its surroundings. The brother then asked him: "How long have you been here, abba?" and the old man said: 'For 72 years now".

Although he admitted openly that not even one of his thoughts rose to the level of Great Anthony's thoughts, he lived in the cave and nobody thought this was defying or fake glory.

The old man was not afraid to show other people that he, too, had sins and made mistakes, either by his way of thinking or by the spiritual advice he gave. Some asked him how to start their holy life, and he answered them that he made mistakes all day long, by what he said and so on. Others asked him what they were supposed to do if they made a mistake, and he answered them that they should rise after each mistake and hope for the Lord's mercy, instead of seeking absolution through their deeds, however spiritually worthy they might seem. Some asked for words of the Gospel to use as a weapon for themselves and for others, but Abba Sisoes did not think that was very useful; instead, he urged them to keep their spirit clean before God and to be serene and without worry under the protection of the Holy Spirit. That was his answer to anything, any time. The old man thought that the Holy Bible had to be studied for one's own spirit, not to provide answers to others. Giving answers? That was a "job" he left to the Holy Spirit.

When the old man was close to his death, disciples and brothers from all the monasteries and mountains came to see him off, to his last resting place, and witnessed his last miracle. In the small cell where he had withdrawn in his old age, he was waiting for his end, watched over by the brothers who were expecting his final words. Suddenly, the saint's face shone bright and he spoke: "Behold, Abba Anthony has come!". Shortly, he said again: "Behold, the company of prophets has come!". His face glowed even more and he said: "Here come the apostles!". Then, he grew even brighter and he seemed to talk to an unseen character. The brothers asked him whom he was talking to, and he answered: "The angels have come for my soul and I'm entreating them to give me a little more time for repentance". The old men said to him: "But you have no need for repentance, Father". And then he answered in tears: "I don't think I have even begun to repent". The fathers were amazed at such humility and understood he had reached perfection. Then, his face suddenly became brighter than the sun and all those present were seized with fear.

The old man muttered: "Behold, the Lord has come and He says: Bring me the chosen vessel which is in the desert". At once, he delivered up his spirit and became like lightening and the whole place filled with a sweet fragrance.

So, the great saint Sisoes led his life between theology and theopraxy, without excelling in one more than in the other and, thus, managing to excel in both.

Asceticism may be defined as the intentional dissatisfaction of bodily needs in view of opening one's mind and spirit to the pleasures and dangers of spiritual life. The human conception is that being in need, lacking basic material things and, in modern times, even lacking more or less luxurious objects, automatically means a lack of fulfilment and of happiness.

The modern or secular, desacralized man is constantly lacking something material, constantly searching to gather material things in order not to acquire the status of wealthy man, but to become fulfilled through objects. Be it expensive food, gold, cars and modern devices, everything leads to the same spiritual dissatisfaction felt by a poor man who lacks the basic things.

The balanced life, consonant with God's Will, can only be obtained by giving up this quantitative way of thinking which, unfortunately, man has got by default these days, because of the epidemics of desacralization of modern world. Asceticism, giving up something is a sort of gate to God. What is given up does not matter, as long as it is something one thinks has a great need for in order to be happy. Asceticism, like sports, must be practised with restraint. Any excess can tear the muscles of the spirit and destroy the concentration needed to permanently watch for dogmatic perils, especially temptations that are coming through virtues, so called right-wing temptations. Asceticism fights the left-wing temptations, the temptations that are coming through vices and, at the same time, cleans the "vessel", the man's spirit, his inner-self and makes it more receptive to the gifts God sends to his "clean vessels".

The life of Saint Sisoes the Great reveals us the "how" that is more difficult and subtle to understand than the theological "what" we focus on. The finesse of his deeds is only surpassed by the finesse of his teachings to the strangers, disciples or wise monks that went to him. The power of his holy way, although skillfully hidden by the saint himself, is revealed in certain moments of his life, such as the following episode from the book "The Sayings of the Fathers of Egypt": "

During a trip, saint Sisoes fell ill and while he was resting in bed, he heard a knock at the door. He then told his disciple to give the one who was knocking this message: "I, Sisoes, in the mountains, I, Sisoes, in bed". And the one who knocked heard this and disappeared." It was the devil who had come to tempt the physically weak Sisoes.

Nobody is born learned and Sisoes had his moments of ascetic excess. One of them was when Sisoes wanted to overcome sleep and, so, hung himself over the precipice of Petra. An angel came to take him down and ordered him not to do that again and not to transmit such teaching to others. Other moments could be considered naive, even childish, had they not been used to teach others, like the many times he would get out of church and rush to his cell, with a quick step, almost running, as if being afraid of something. Some of the people who saw him would say: he is possessed by the devil. But Saint Sisoes, doing God's work, paid no attention to what they said about him.

Although both the ascetic successes and the less successful trials show him as a skilful and courageous ascetic, in the end, we see in the saint's words and deeds that the importance he gave to asceticism is calculated in his theopraxy.

Thus, in several episodes related to food, we see that Sisoes did not object when he was invited to drink wine or to eat when he was fasting, because he did not want to offend the others or to have fake glory. He did not risk to betray, by his refusal, the successes in his ascetic life, but at the same time, he rightly measured his actions, according to the circumstances:

"Once an offering took place on the mountain of Abba Anthony and a vessel of wine was found in the offering. Taking a small bottle and a cup, one of the elders brought it to Abba Sisoes and gave it to him, and he drank it. Likewise, he took a second cup and drank it. And he offered him a third, but he did not take it, saying: Stop, brother, or do you not know that this is from Satan?"

"They used to say about Abba Sisoes the Theban that he never ate bread. During the Easter Festival the brethren came to him, and having made excuses they entreated him to eat with them; and he answered and said, "I will do one [of two] things; I will either eat bread and bread alone, or I will eat of the meats which ye have boiled." And they said unto him," Then eat bread only". And he did so.

They used to say that Abba Sisoes the Theban was wont to dwell among the reeds of Arsania, where there was, at some distance from him, an old man who was sick; and when he heard [of it] he was distressed, for he fasted two days at a time, and that day was the day on which he ought not to eat. And he said in his mind, "What shall I do? For perhaps the brethren will compel me to eat, and if I wait [to go to the old man]

until to-morrow perhaps he will be dead. I can only do this. I will go, but will not break the law and eat"; so he went, and he ate not, and he did not break the rule of life which [he observed] for God's sake."
The Sayings of the Fathers of Egypt

Asceticism, through its sacrifices, brought Abba Sisoes both physical and spiritual fulfilment. He subdued his body to his spirit, but avoiding the traps of fake glory, which can also come from focusing too much on the ascetic rules.

A young monk said to Abba Sisoes: "Abba, what should I do? I fell." The elder answered: "Get up!" The monk said: "I got up and I fell again!" The elder replied: "Get up again!" But the young monk asked: "For how long should I get up when I fall?" "Until your death," answered Abba Sisoes. "For a man heads to his judgment either fallen or getting back up again."

The end of the life of Sisoes the Great with a lightening of holy light shows us not only that the old man was worthy to live in the cave of Saint Anthony the Great, but also that God welcomes those who do not despair and keep getting back up.

This also shows us that asceticism brings fulfilment, for who doesn't wish to end their life with the heavenly escort that welcomed the Saint, with the whole Old and New Testament along with the Lord Himself welcoming him to Heaven with an explosion of holy light as a crown for his successful life?

We wouldn't be surprised to learn that the Patriarch Adam himself was proud of that moment, like a father who sees his dream fulfilled by his son.

Looking through the eyes of the Dark Angel
Evil and Its Expressions

The spiritual quality of man is given by the quality of the evil that resides within him.

If a man has all the possible virtues and only one vice, even an insignificant one, the quality of that man's spirit will be dictated by that one vice. The saints themselves had failures and made mistakes, which is precisely why they said that all the sins they'd made turned them into sinners, but all the good they'd done before God did not turn them into saints, despite the graceful gifts God bestowed on them as an assurance that their spiritual effort was well received.

Hence, man should work daily on improving the quality of his spirit, fighting against the thoughts and vices that pull him down.

"The eye is the lamp of the body. So, if your eye is healthy, your whole body will be full of light, but if your eye is bad, your whole body will be full of darkness. If then the light in you is darkness, how great is the darkness!" Matthew 6, 22-23

But what happens if man does not actively fight the evil inside him? The first thing that a spiritually careless man loses is **empathy**.

The ability of putting oneself in someone else's shoes, of thinking for a second of someone else's feelings is the first victim of a hardened heart. When, whether intentionally or not, one forgets about his brother's feelings and starts judging him according to his own reasoning, empathy disappears and only with great pains does it come back. For the oppressor, the action itself does not hold the same value as for the oppressed, and so, the oppressor will be much less affected by the consequences of his actions. He will continue to oppress, to cause pain until it is time for him to feel pain. It is then and only then that he reconsiders his gestures, his actions, and even his words down to the details of the way he looked upon the others, his whole body and spirit being transfigured by empathy.

The way in which one looks upon the world, i.e. caring vs. indifferent, loving vs. judging, candid vs. sly, innocent vs. pervert, is defined by the set of values and knowledge one has undertaken as true and worth following. Based on these values, man looks upon the entire spectrum of creation, from the microcosm to the macrocosm, with preconceptions, ideas more or less processed by him and adjusted so as to serve his ultimate purpose.

As long as the chosen purpose is damaging and ephemeral, contrary to the divine laws of love and respect, the preconceptions and the actions based on them will be expressions of evil and will choke that man's soul in the darkness of sin, of the absence of divine grace

LACK OF EMPATHY

Some people completely lack empathy and their heart is hardened by all kinds of means, some ideological, others factual like wealth, high status, fleeting power over other people. As the very purpose of their life is impure, it will choke them in this hardness for the rest of their lives. The Lord will signal them in many ways, but as a rule, for exceptions have been and will continue to be, their hardness of heart continues until they pass away. This is possible because, although these people have access to education or sufficient experiences to learn empathy, they do not accept empathy as something worth developing deep down inside them. Some, powerful people of their time or even philosophers (see F. Nietzsche in his work "Thus spoke Zarathustra"), see empathy as a weakness of the soul and do not acknowledge the power and courage of this virtue. On the contrary, they strive with all their might to become insensitive for purely ideological reasons, thus educating themselves to be real monsters to their fellow beings and preaching the "benefits" of this practice, to others, as well, benefits which almost always seem to be of a material or selfish nature.

Other people are guided towards the lack of empathy by their hate and envy of their fellow beings, whether we speak about individual experiences, or an ideological and religious rule they have chosen to govern their lives; sometimes, for both reasons, the individual experiences - poverty, reprimand, lack of status - leading to a secular ideology or criminal religious dogma.

Both categories of people above look upon the kind and compassionate people with an even greater hatred than they look upon those similar to them. The sly ones would wish to take advantage of the compassion and kindness of the considerate people, while the tyrannical ones would like to change their conceptions, even by force, through all kinds of terrible challenges. Thus, both categories find pleasure in mocking the concept of empathy, in fighting the concept and its gifts: compassion, the joy of charity, interest in other people's vertical development, etc.

All these people's hearts are hardened and few of them will come to reason at some point in their lives, enough to change the way they live, they think and, later on, the way they act.

UNEDUCATED EMPATHY

Another category of people is represented by those with **uneducated empathy**, i.e. empathy that is not disciplined or filtered through the wise values that a man who is aware of his spiritual path will try to build throughout his lifetime.

Emotional people, who are led (surprised) by emotions rather than experiment them consciously, in a disciplined manner, as a result of life rules, will apply or not the gifts of empathy depending on the circumstances, the other people's appreciation, the fear of the authorities, their interest in the moment, hence factors outside the solid, wise values they lack and search with all their being. These people have the possibility to either become wise or run away from the wisdom they are supposed to acquire, and it all depends on how they receive the signals that God sends to all the people: physical pain, similar traumatic experiences, poverty, injustice, etc.

I said that these people are swallowed by the darkness within them because they do not recognise it enough to fight it and stop being led by it. This is why their uneducated empathy can be manipulated by others so as to diminish and even perish forever, these people allowing themselves to be convinced by ideas that either justify their cowardly actions or scare them and repress the good within. The great majority of the population of Earth is included in this category.

EDUCATED EMPATHY

We've come to the people with **educated empathy**, which constantly increases and produces many gifts, like material and spiritual compassion, the joy of charity, of justice, of love, etc., which they use to bring comfort to their fellow beings. This category of people has attained disciplined empathy through intellectual, spiritual and even physical effort, by educating their spirit through the fire of the ideological and theological equations that they solved with strain, faith and, many times, sacrifice or even sacrifice, in extreme cases.

An example of educated empathy is given by the Saviour, as shown below:

"Greater love has no one than this, that he lay down his life for his friends." John 15, 13

These people think in universal, divine terms, the only terms worth accepting among the values that plant in us empathy, the divine instrument for our godliness.

Saint Symeon the New Theologian showed the dimension of this empathy:

"I have seen a man who [...] for those who fell in word or deed or who persisted in evil, he grievously mourned and lamented as if he himself were truly responsible for all these things and had to account for them and suffer punishment. I have seen yet another who was so zealous and filled with desire for the salvation of his brethren that he often implored God, who loves man, with all his souls and with warm tears that either they might be saved or else that he be *condemned with them. His attitude was like that of Moses and indeed of God Himself in that he did not in any way wish to be saved alone. Because he was spiritually bound to them by holy love in the Holy Spirit, he did not want to enter into the Kingdom of Heaven itself if that meant he would be separated from them."*

Saint Symeon the New Theologian: The Catechetical Discourses
Discourse 8: "Of Perfect Love and What It Is"

EVIL IN ITS INDIVIDUAL FORM

Evil can take much more brutal forms than the lack of empathy. Absolute horrors take place everywhere in the world because of the specific wish of several members of the human race, members by name only, as they are similar to devils in actions and thoughts. Whether the world knows them as criminals, pedophiles or does not know them at all yet or may not know them until the Judgment Day, these people have a love relationship with evil: first, they court it, then they experiment it, and later they reach the extremes of evil, as if trying to test the limits of society, of their fellow beings and, eventually, their own limits in causing, accepting and enduring evil.

To them, evil is a field of knowledge, of delight, of negative spiritual evolution. These people are not so much concerned by the quantity of evil they can cause like the tyrants, who do evil rather based on calculations, but by the quality of the malefic act they engage in, whether or not aware of the evil spirits that watch and help them.

Evil people find pleasure in perverting innocent victims, in destroying hope (a divine gift), which the victim can lose gradually during the evil act, until despair settles in, as vividly intended by the criminal in the first place.

The criminal feels like a sort of priest, theologian, philosopher of evil and its expressions, finding justification in the act of becoming acquainted with evil at:

Philosophical level – The criminal wants to test the extremes, to know the essence of the Evil and, those who think of themselves as researchers only also want to know, by comparison, the essence of Good;

Evolutional level – He wants to change his human status into one similar to that of the black angels, he wants to know unlimited power, without remorse or negative consequences on him;

Universal level – He has associated with the devil's army and actively fights the Lord and His creation, finding joy in destroying this creation and so, in his vision, a piece of God.

The evil act can be merely intended and never carried into effect throughout that man's life; yet, spiritually, he will be able and willing to turn his thoughts into actions, his simulations into practice, his vision into reality. The Gospel calls these people "blood shedders".

EVIL APPLIED AT MASS SCALE

Some of these malefic people get to positions of power either by chance or by design.

Those who carefully plan and act are the **Tyrants**.

To become a tyrant, the criminal is not satisfied with just creating the conditions for researching evil, but enforces Evil at mass level. To this end, he will create the lying, but rationally strong ideologies needed to establish the conditions for his research laboratory.

Some, like the Roman emperor Caligula, relied on the quantity of evil they did in their endeavour to turn from simple men into gods,or supermen. Caligula hoped to become a god before his death, which disheartened and pushed him to despair, by forcing all the subjects of the Roman Empire to bring offerings to him, as to a god. This also explains his effort of placing his statue in God's Temple in Jerusalem, which eventually did not occur due to Caligula's premature death.

Even then, the tyrant's hunger for ideologies that would justify his actions and would satisfy his wish to change the entire nation according to his vision was obvious. The cult of personality is nothing more than the tyrant's assurance that the world will forcibly accept his vision and, at the same time, an instrument to identify those who truly oppose his work.

After identifying those who oppose themselves, the tyrant changes the weak and the coward and eliminates the strong, lest they should be models of courage to others. The remaining population controlled by the tyrant serves only to nourish and enhance his joy of seeing his vision "in the flesh". He requires them to praise him and sing songs to him, while he laughs at all his subjects, showing respect for nothing and no one.

EVIL IN IDEOLOGIES

Modern history has showed us yet another time that *"the whole world lies under the power of the evil one"* 1 John 5, 19.

But where can one better see the power of the devil in the world if not in the ideologies that are tools of evil?

Any ideology that involves denigrating the word of the Lord and teaches the common man to ignore the spiritual life can be resembled to the experience of men before the Flood, when all of them thought Noah was crazy and laughed at him and at his efforts of obeying the Lord. No modern ideology succeeds in explaining the creation of the world or life after death with the same authority that we see in God's words from the Holy Book.

Thus, modern ideologies only focus on destroying God's word and on regulating the society according to the agenda of the originator of such ideologies with regard to controlling people. Usually, this agenda begins by having an economic nature like distributing the resources of earth or something like that and ends up having a social nature like controlling the humanity to achieve the stated or not stated goal.

All modern ideologies are atheist because, by reducing or annulling God's role of ordering the world and the human relations through His laws, they undertake an authority they do not have. By usurping the supreme authority, they offend the very way in which Creation was designed and brought into being. Being atheist, these ideologies have as clear objective to fight the notion of divinity, not because they seek the truth, but because they would be destroyed if the truth was God, as declared by the Saviour. It is hence proven that these ideologies, created by beings who are neither omniscient, omnipotent, nor eternal, are in fact mistaken in what they preach to be the truth.

This shows that the source of modern ideologies is pure evil, which uses these tools to fight the minds of people who still believe in God.

Naturally, by using the data retrieved by men from the study of creation (i.e. from science), ideologies interpret everything so as to contradict the history of creation of the world and man, as told by God and later supported by the Prophets, the Apostles and the Saviour Himself, through the Holy Spirit. An example is given in the parable of the tenants of the vineyard, told in the Gospel of Matthew. This parable tells of the farmers who rented a rich man's vineyard and then did not want to give him the fruits at harvest time; instead, they beat and killed the owner's faithful servants and even his son, the heir of the vineyard, like thieves and murderers:

"This is the heir. Come, let's kill him and take his inheritance." Matthew 21, 38

The inheritance is the human race itself. The ideologies that fight this inheritance and try to usurp the Lord are the real aggressors of humankind, most times disguised as saviours. Their origin is bad because they come from the Evil One and he uses pieces of truth along with lies to make the people spiritually careless, and, so, weak, to turn them for eternity towards evil instead of towards God's loving laws. The Evil One knows he has no authority over the truth, but he lies. Believing a lie over the truth shows weak faith in the Lord. The trick is easy and does not work with the souls of the faithful men, but it does work with those who already rebel against God and accept any justification, any ideology, as long as it serves their purpose!

FIGHTING THE EVIL

Eradicating evil from people at the individual level and then at the social level is the object of the entire Christian literature, the life of Jesus Christ being the main model of a Christian life, as the Saviour came into the world and said:

"In this world you will have trouble. But take heart! I have overcome the world." John 16:33

Since the coming of the Saviour, men have had the chance to "overcome the world" and, thus, the evil that comes from the world, by using all the gifts of the divine grace bestowed by the Holy Spirit, the first one being faith. Due to man's faith in the Lord and to his sincere search for the Lord, man will please the Lord who, this way, will see that man is ready for many other gifts waiting to be offered to him when the time is right for his soul. Apart from having faith, the Saviour's advice to men was and still is: *"Study the Scriptures"!* John 5:39.

Not knowing the Scriptures leads to error; consequently, by reading them, modern men will find their salvation, as the Saviour said: *"You are in error because you do not know the Scriptures or the power of God."* Matthew 22, 29

Naturally, when reading these Scriptures, man should not have the attitude of Pontius Pilate regarding the Truth. The search for the divine message must be done with faith and an open heart, otherwise, if read without faith, the Scriptures are no use:

*"But since you do not believe what he (*Moses, the faithful servant*) wrote, how are you going to believe what I say?"* John 5, 39

Thus, by faithfully reading the Holy Scriptures and by trusting God's words, man will receive God's gifts and he will become strong in the fight with evil, being taught step by step what to do to turn his weak, evil-oriented nature after his Fall, to the condition of being a son of God.

The mature faithful man does not stumble on the ideologies come from the Evil One, as he cannot be lied to with pieces of truth. Through the Holy Spirit, he has access to the whole truth and so he can see where the lie creeps in the modern ideological discourse.

DUTY TO VANQUISH EVIL

The evil within man is a direct consequence of no

longer obeying the Lord. Thus, man has the duty to fight evil, not only because he wishes to redeem himself individually, but mostly because he thus fulfils the divine justice and allows God to fix him, working as actively as possible, along with God, to this end.

The man who fixes himself has the duty to fix others, as well, working alongside the Lord, just like those who help propagate Evil in the world consciously or unconsciously work alongside Satan for their purpose. The fight is hard and it begins at a personal level, but it must be carried on by strengthening the correct principles and by predicating them to the world.

The love of people is not a duty that the faithful man must somehow accommodate in his ideology, but the natural condition of the spirit itself, as it was created, without sin, full of love and of the Lord's gifts. This virtue is deemed held when experienced on a daily basis. Thus, it helps spreading the truth of God not through words, by through actions which speak for themselves. The love of people comes through grace, due to man's faith and obedience to the divine laws:

"God's love has been poured into our hearts through the Holy Spirit who has been given to us." Romans 5, 5

Man becomes acquainted with the acts of faith by reading the Scriptures. He then must find within him, little by little, the power to apply them. Once man has acquired faith, he must make shy, but firm steps towards acquiring empathy towards his fellow beings, towards loving the creatures of God and helping them at the same time he helps himself.

After empathy, with some effort, he will eventually get to the utter medicine against evil: love. The Holy Spirit shows clearly the ephemeral nature of ideologies and the importance of the virtue of love, through the words of the Apostle Paul:

"If I speak in the tongues of men and of angels, but have not love, I am a noisy gong or a clanging cymbal. And if I have prophetic powers, and understand all mysteries and all knowledge, and if I have all faith, so as to remove mountains, but have not love, I am nothing. Love never ends. As for prophecies, they will pass away; as for tongues, they will cease; as for knowledge, it will pass away. For we know in part and we prophesy in part, but when the perfect comes, the partial will pass away." 1 Corinthians 13, 1-2, 8-10

This medicine heals everything very efficiently. It is greater than any virtue or power of the opposing evil:

"So now faith, hope, and love abide, these three; but the greatest of these is love." 1 Corinthians 13, 13

By fighting the evil within us and in the world, by never losing our faith in God and His laws, we win the fight from the very beginning and we remain winners until we finish it, because we fulfil God's commandment of becoming sons of God on earth: *"God is love, and whoever abides in love abides in God, and God abides in him."* 1 John 4, 16

Both evil and its expressions are part of the "old sky" and the "old earth", desecrated by the sins of the devils and of men, therefore evil is ephemeral.

God's judgement will come along with a "new sky" and a "new earth", when evil will come to its end, losing its power for ever and becoming inexistent in the eternity of God and His faithful creatures.

21

"Vanitas Vanitatum!"

The only engine of all man's enterprises throughout his lifetime is **the final purpose** for which he undertakes all of his actions. If this purpose is illusory, fake, deceiving, man will despair either before finding a real purpose, worth pursuing, or while pursuing his illusory purpose and, especially, after finding its faultiness and futility.

If the purpose chosen is not real and eternal, Man's despair will surge with time irrespective of his wish to pursue a specific illusory purpose or no purpose at all. Hence, he will not be able to prevent the feeling of despair from overwhelming him and from eventually destroying his wish of pursuing his illusory and unsatisfying goal. Therefore, man's purpose must be defined as valid and infinite, in temporal terms and not only, right from the beginning, so that it may escape the horrors of ephemerality and insufficiency and to be able to inspire man beyond his small earthly life.

This purpose must take into account the material, mental and spiritual factors of Creation, which could be defined as everything outside the Essence of God.

The first factor, the material one, illustrates through its elements many of the paths we should not take. In 1798, Thomas Malthus stipulated a theorem regarding the development of the human population, showing that sometime in the nearer or further future, mankind will run out of sufficient resources for supporting its growth and, later, even for surviving. This theorem was based on the fact that mankind will always need food and that men and women will always find a way to procreate, no matter how a society is organised. The basis of resources, which, in Malthus's theorem, is the planet Earth, will end up being insufficient and will be consumed beyond its power of regeneration. Thinkers of many literary movements have thought of solutions for breaking this barrier. We will select and expose only the most daring solutions, for example: populating other planets or creating artificial habitats outside the planet Earth, and we will take our mental exercise even further, pushing these solutions to the extremes.

Even if men managed to populate all the planets in all the planetary systems, in all the galaxies of the Universe and even fill all the space between the galaxies with artificial habitats, using the energy of the entire Universe, of all the space bodies, including the interstellar or intergalactic dust, as well as of other material energies, more hidden now to our scientific sight, so that they may successfully grow and develop, sooner or later the Universe would still run out of energy, the Universe maximum entropy.

In conclusion, the quantitative growth is an unsustainable model even in conditions of maximum technological efficiency, technology being merely a form of organising and using the energy of the Universe.

Mankind does not have a well-defined purpose in terms of its evolution, this philosophical-mental "place" being still an unknown that no philosophical system knew how to fill with something significant and inspiring enough.

The second factor is of a mental nature and it involves two dilemmas: a material one and an ideational one.

The material dilemma shows us that, no matter how much knowledge we could gather in our more or less developed brain, we will eventually be unable to acquire any more ideas because of the lack of space in the cranial mass. There is a reason why we cannot recite the entire library ever written by mankind, namely the physical limits of the human brain. Once again, we will push this idea to the extremes for the sake of this mental exercise and we will infer that, even if the brain of a single man were as big as the entire Universe, it still couldn't contain all the ideas that the brain would think at a given time and, thus, omniscience becomes impossible. Consequently, the purpose of mankind cannot be gathering knowledge without discrimination.

But if we try to discriminate and select the ideas we wish to have in our brain, in our mind, we end up having **the second dilemma: which ideas are valuable enough to keep in our mind and according to which criteria do we select them?**

This dilemma of ideas, spiritual in its essence, means asking ourselves why we should select an idea to the detriment of another when we've reached the conclusion that omniscience is not the purpose of humanity. In the end, any idea that just postpones and does not solve the material dilemma presented here above (i.e. that growth is finite and meaningless) is meant to fail and should not be kept in our limited brain. But even if we remembered the most important knowledge about the micro and macro Universe, along with the most efficient analyses of this knowledge, such information would eventually be useless as it would not change the failing orbit of the human spirit. In the end, we will get bored of controlling the Universe and, with nothing more to do, to aim for, to watch, we will contemplate mass suicide.

We now get to **the third factor, the spiritual one,** which holds the solution to this purpose exercise.

The human spirit does not depend on the mental or bodily capacity to succeed in evolving towards a superior form. The spiritual powers are energies that come from God and must be interpreted with the tools He gave us and that operate only when we are in symbiosis with God. Man can only evolve together with the Omniscient, Omnipotent Being, who contains within **infinite resources of any kind**. Moreover, man does not have any direction of evolution other than towards the Essence of God and he is helped by the energies with which God guides us so that He may reveal Himself to man. The final purpose is not even to know God in its entirety, as this is firstly impossible and secondly it would mean that, after getting to know God, there would still be another purpose for man to reach.

The correct end-purpose of man is to have access to God, which is possible only with God's help, so that, once the symbiosis is achieved, man could start **his infinite climbing up to God**. This purpose cannot be completed, as it is directly related to God's infinite attributes. If man chooses another purpose, he will sooner or later face the failure of that purpose, both in terms of ideals and of completion.

Thus, in the face of a clear and error-free road, man will be able to enjoy all the aspects of life, both material and spiritual, without ever tasting the cup of despair, unmercifully offered to all those who step off this path.

The Fight between Cain's Sons and Abel's Sons

"Cain spoke to Abel his brother. And when they were in the field, **Cain rose up against his brother Abel and killed him.***"* Genesis 4:8

Let's call it as it is: Abel has got sons!

When God speaks about the blood shedders, He speaks about the sons of Cain, the one who killed the first man out of envy and hatred. But Abel has got sons, as well. They are today and always have been those who fight for justice; they are Abel's blood screaming to God from the earth.

Throughout history, we have seen kind, wise men, morally superior to those focusing only on subduing others, who fought the sons of Cain. The kind people try by means of mercy and common sense, politeness and goodwill, to uplift the hearts of the ignorant to their vision of a brotherly life.

Cain's sons utterly despise the virtues above, seeing in them only weakness and discomfort, not wishing to show even for a second their natural vulnerability as humans, and pushing their criminal agenda without considering its painful consequences. Their agenda is based on the wish for power, for undeserved authority, taken by force, a wish to subdue many of their human fellows because they are not satisfied with just 10 or 100, but want millions of slaves, if possible.

According to the Holy Scriptures, Nimrod was the first men after the Flood who "started to be powerful on earth" and who wished to gather people around him, not to benefit them, but to have them serve him. He had a clear agenda of stealing humankind away from the purposes given by God and of using it for new purposes, designed by Nimrod, and maybe also by others around him, for new ideals that aimed to fight the power of the Lord.

Before the Flood, there had been the mighty men and the Nephilim, offspring of the sons of God, who came from the seed of Seth, and of the daughters of men, who came from the seed of Cain. These mighty men and Nephilim had done so much wrong on earth that the entire world had become full of wickedness and unimaginably perverted.

God was compelled to punish them visibly: *"The Nephilim were on the earth in those days, and also afterward, when the sons of God came in to the daughters of man and they bore children to them. These were **the mighty men who were of old, the men of renown.**"* (Here, "mighty men" should be understood as tyrants, people who use their power to make themselves a name.) *"The LORD saw that the wickedness of man was great in the earth, and that every intention of the thoughts of his heart was only evil continually. And the LORD was sorry that he had made man on the earth, and it grieved him to his heart. So the LORD said, "I will blot out man whom I have created from the face of the land, man and animals and creeping things and birds of the heavens, for I am sorry that I have made them." But Noah found favor in the eyes of the LORD."* Genesis 6, 4-8

Ham, a son of Noah, had had Cush who, in his turn, had had Nimrod, the first man who wanted to be above all men on account of his force. He taught them to actively fight the will of God, building with them a tower meant to survive a potential flood, thus trying to limit God's options to punish the entire humankind.

His final purpose was to gain independence from the power of God and to escape the obedience of His laws.

The rebellion against the authority of God and against the men vested with His authority, for example patriarchs, prophets, etc., started right after mankind was saved from the Flood. Ham, one of the three sons saved from the Flood along with Noah, undermined Noah's authority by attempting to disgrace his father before his two other sons, Shem and Japheth. Ham saw by chance *"the nakedness of his father and told his two brothers outside"* (Genesis 9:22), so he tried to involve his brothers in his evil work of undermining Noah's authority. But Shem and Japheth gave their father **respect**, by covering his nakedness without looking at it. The consequence of this sinful deed after the Flood was that Noah cursed Canaan, the son of Ham and, thus, Canaan's descendents were subjected by Shem's descendents in the war for the Holy Land promised to Abraham, direct descendent of Shem.

But the other sons of Ham, too, had descendents who fought the sons of Shem. For example, from the son Egypt came the Philistines with whom the Jewish people fought hard. From Cush came Nimrod who, being strong (*"He was the first on earth to be a mighty man"* - I Chronicles 1:10), taught the people to rise against God's will and tried to intimidate and manipulate them into joining under his will. Nobody could be considered mighty on earth without first inspiring fear, so without actively intimidating. This is why the people of old feared only God and lived as they could in peace, without worrying about being subdued by others, without chiefs above them, to serve the way they served God.

But after Cain's kill for envy and Lamech's kill for a simple bruise, Nimrod, after the Flood, made hunting (killing, destroying) his most famous "virtue". Thus, Nimrod started causing other people to fear and respect his power, both by his actions and by his successes to such an extent that a saying including his name has crossed the entire ancient history until nowadays, as showed by the following excerpt from the Holy Scriptures:

"Cush was the father of Nimrod, who became a mighty warrior on the earth (a tyrant).

He was a mighty hunter before the LORD; *that is why it is said, "Like Nimrod, a mighty hunter before the* LORD*."* Genesis 10, 8-9

Instead of obedience to God with wisdom, peace and serenity, Nimrod offered the strength of his arm and plans of rebellion in the land ruled by him.

"The beginning of his kingdom was Babel, Erech, Accad, and Calneh, in the land of Shinar. From that land he went into Assyria and built Nineveh, Rehoboth-Ir, Calah, and Resen between Nineveh and Calah; that is the great city." Genesis 10, 10-12

Thus, as son of Noah's only son fallen from grace, Nimrod is a rebel, just like Cain, and Nimrod's actions and ideology will be repeated throughout history by different sons of Cain, who will not stop at anything to prove to the world their cruelty, a "quality" highly valued by them. This quality is necessary for ruling the world with an iron hand and none of those who seek power over others will lack it.

Since Nimrod, all the people who looked for power have wanted it so that they can subdue their brothers, and not so as to become closer to God. This is why any human ideology or falsely religious ideology adopted by the powerful will contain the elements of crime and domination over their subjects. Nimrod's ideologies (all the heads of the hydra) must also contain a strong element of rebellion either against God, denying even His existence, or against the salvaging laws given by Him to mankind. Hence, these ideologies will teach against the right faith, the right obedience to God on earth.

The utmost examples that shows how absolutely opposed Nimrod's ideologies are to God's message and laws are given by Jesus Christ Himself in His message:

"But I say to you, love your enemies and pray for those who persecute you." Matthew 5, 44.

Christ's message is a more complete confirmation of the message in the Old Testament, transmitted through Moses:

"You shall not take vengeance or bear a grudge against the sons of your own people, but **you shall love your neighbor as yourself***: I am the LORD."* Leviticus 19, 18

Under the reign of Cain's sons, "the blood shedders", ruthless people, the concept of justice was gradually changed, until it became a joke. Thus, we see aberrations, such as: the rich people's taxes are lower or inexistent compared to the taxes to be paid by the common people, the rich become richer and the poor lose their dignity in sheer poverty, to the delight of the rich who devilishly enjoy this and push the poor even further in the loss of any dignity they may have left.

The ruling class dares breaking the law overtly, without fear of the justice system, which they control as they please, as shown by the numerous artful tricks a lawyer can invoke to make a client look innocent after committing an outrageous crime. One of the many recent examples of this "justice" that makes a joke on the victims and weakens people's faith in it includes a father killing his small children to get back at the mother, while the justice, without any mental deficiency evidence, rules in favour of "temporary insanity" and gives him back his freedom after only a few psychological tests that, naturally, conclude the father is safe to be reintegrated into society.

The concept of justice and of equality before justice is not the only one mocked by the sons of Cain. They attack the very concept of right to life of the unborn children and they plead for all kinds of criminal liberties which men, who hated the divine laws on procreation, accept as the letter of the law, thus creating the conditions for a war between the human law, which has no absolute authority and, as such, is false and opportunistic and the divine law, which has all the Creator's absolute and unchanging authority.

At society level, the sons of Cain use their libertine ideologies to tempt and manipulate the weak people and propose a freedom that defies all the laws of God. This freedom can be paralleled by the "30 silvers" for which Judah sold the Saviour as this "treason" transforms into Judas all those who sell their obedience to the eternal laws to find an unlimited, chaotic and debauchee freedom to be used for their satanic purposes against the Lord. The original rebellion, the Devil's, is thus replicated by these people with the utmost passion and it brings to their souls the same satanic hatred against the divine message.

And yet, despite all their desperate efforts of freeing themselves from the laws of God, they are seized with every passing day by a state of acedia, a condition of the soul consisting in horrible boredom, spiritual dissatisfaction, and chronic despair, which grows more and more intolerable, as **the reward of peace of mind and heart does not lie in this demonic freedom.**

In contrast with the demonic attitude of Cain's sons to the love of the Heavenly Father is the attitude of Abel's sons, people who first of all love the Truth, then the Creation and look upon their fellow human beings with kindness and respect. Even when they fight the rebels, they do it with love, not with hate.

The sons of Abel try to conquer the sons of Cain

with their ideas and virtues that come from the grace of God, not by force. Their life is a living sermon that focuses not on judging their fellow human beings, but on rising them through the right teachings. Nothing makes them happier than succeeding in saving their brothers from the madness they entered and in changing their souls from black to white, from overt enemies to loving brothers.

There are many examples of beautiful lives of people who try to live nicely, according to God's will, and which have been acknowledged in the books about the saints and the martyrs of Jesus Christ's church. There are even more lives that have not been acknowledged or known by the written history of humanity, lives that pleased both God and those who had the chance to know such wonderful people. They were fathers and sons, mothers and daughters, masters and servants, friends and strangers who brought joy to those around them through small and great gestures, some of which maybe changed the history or only brought a smile and hope on the face of someone terrorised by the darkness of the world. They are "the salt of the earth" of which speaks Jesus Christ (Matthew 5:13); they give pan-spiritual value to the entire humankind by obeying the Lord's laws, but mostly by the finesse and spiritual strength they have reached, despite all the obstacles thrown by the sons of Cain.

After all, each soul has a value identical to that of the other souls. Therefore, we will not stress the importance of a good soul compared to a less good soul. All the sons of Cain are called to become sons of Abel and, as such, pleasing to the Lord. Nobody is forgotten and the gate to this change remains open until man's last breath. But how beautiful and wonderful it is for a soul to return to the Lord way before the death of the body! This way, the soul has got time to do some spiritually good actions and to grow into a spiritual maturity that honours it when it starts its journey to Eternity, to the real life that only then begins. Moreover, the joy of those around them in seeing this return to the natural life under the laws of the Lord brings hope upon such people.

When the Berlin Wall was built after the Second World War and this criminal construction, which became a grave for many people in their quest for freedom and normality, was still at the beginning, there took place lots of stories that bring hope in man's inner kindness.

One of these stories can be an inspiration to us today:

The wall was defended by border checkpoints, served by soldiers who watched that no one crossed without a pass. This wall stretched without discrimination across streets, buildings and backyards of people's homes. On one of the main streets, a German soldier from East Berlin (which was under the Soviet occupation), who was in charge of guarding the checkpoint, was watching as people on the other side of the wall, in West Berlin, were trying to talk to him and soften his heart. The families of the people in the West had been separated as many of their members had been caught unaware by the construction and rules of this Wall and were now trapped in East Berlin, unable to go back. So they were talking to this soldier with the hope that they could turn him from a criminal tool of the communist system into a man who listened to his heart.

At some point, the soldier began to feel the change within and the crowd in the free Berlin must have seen it in his eyes. Women with bags, men passing by, youngsters, they all started shouting words of encouragement and saying: "Come to us, jump over the wall, cross the border, freedom is right here, waiting for you! Come here!" When the choir of encouragements reached paroxysm, the soldier threw away his gun, stepped on the barbed wire and jumped over the Wall, his face a mix of fear and joy of complete freedom. This epic moment was captured by a professional photographer, by the grace of God. The private's name was Conrad Schumann.

Private Schumann, who was only 19 years old at the time that picture was taken, decided to escape to the West on account of two things. The first one was that, the same morning, he had seen a little girl offering flowers through the barbed wire to her mother who was trapped in East Berlin. The second one was that the people had called out to him to ally with the forces of light and leave the forces of darkness behind.

The professional photographer who captured the soldier's jump over the Wall had the privilege of taking the symbol-picture of the Cold War, a picture that utterly expresses the humanity of those in the oppressed side of the Iron Curtain. This **act of passage** caught in a picture helped people on both sides of the Curtain to acknowledge their humanity and to hope that one day they would escape the tyranny of Cain's sons who held the power at that time, more forcefully than in other times. Although the tyranny in East Berlin was one of the harshest back then, the city being occupied by Soviet soldiers and Germans who had betrayed their country, nation and God and who used intimidation and pressure against the population, private Conrad crossed the border from the hell where, had he stayed, he would have been forced to commit murders against the humanity, to the heaven of a free man's life. With such passages across "the wall" separating the "bad sons" from the "good sons", those who bring hope to mankind become more numerous.

The beauty of the human spirit does not consist in what it could do, but in what it actually does at a given time. Let us try to bring more beauty to ourselves and those around us by multiplying the kind actions that our heart subtly encourages us to make. These actions are truly divine and, as soon as we make them, we become for a short moment sons of Abel, who was so pleasing to God through his deeds and sacrifices, that God Himself named him **righteous**.

By persevering in such actions, we will fulfill the divine justice, showing that **Cain, too, may become Abel** as God only reprimanded Cain, but wished he would go back to his spiritually beautiful nature, and that nobody in this world is without hope of entering the eternal life with their heads held up high and their hearts filled with joy.

"Then the LORD said to Cain:

Why are you angry? Why is your face downcast? If you do what is right, will you not be accepted? But if you do not do what is right, sin is crouching at your door;

It desires to have you, **but you must rule over it.***"* Genesis 4, 6-7

Death, God's Mercy towards Man

Back when man was created, the initial plan was to have a creature born out of love and sheer joy, who would crown God's creation by the sensibility of his relation with God; a creature who, right from the beginning, was given the chance to be more than the powerful angels, to be God's co-creator of a piece of the universe, over which God had him rule:

"Let us make man in our image, after our likeness. And let them have dominion [...]."

This creature (i.e. man) received a frail body and a complex nature, in the image of God (*"So God created man in his own image, in the image of God he created him"*), being made up of three parts:

1. the Body, which is the material part,
2. the Soul, the affective part,

3. and the Spirit, the rational part and keeper of the godly principles and laws, master of the other two parts.

We see in the writings of the Apostle Paul, the man taken to the Third Heaven (2 Corinthians 12, 1-6), that the Spirit and the Soul, although tightly connected and intertwined, are still distinct parts of man's structure, which received different names in the speech of the great apostle of mankind:

*"For the word of God is living and active, sharper than any two-edged sword, **piercing to the division of soul and of spirit**, of joints and of marrow, and discerning the thoughts and intentions of the heart. And no creature is hidden from his sight, but all are naked and exposed to the eyes of him to whom we must give account."* Hebrews 4, 12-13

*"Now may the God of peace himself sanctify you completely, **and may your whole spirit and soul and body** be kept blameless at the coming of our Lord Jesus Christ."* 1 Thessalonians 5, 23

Although any comparison between the structure of the Holy Trinity and Man may suffer deeply from the lack of information on the Divine Mystery of the Holy Trinity, we can still wonder at the sign of the cross and how it was chosen as the main Christian sign from the beginning of the primary church. The sign of the cross places God the Father above everyone, the Son, who descended upon earth in a human body, under Him and the Holy Spirit in the middle. The Holy Spirit comes from the Father and co-works with the Son according to God's will, being named the Comforter by the Son. Thus the sign of the cross seems to seal the union of the Father and Son through the Holly Spirit. So, if we were to make a parallel, the Son would symbolise the body consecrated by the Holy Spirit, which symbolise the affective part, the soul, and they would both obey the Father, the ruling part, the spirit, showing us how to begin our understanding of the Divine Mystery of Holy Trinity.

The body, although fragile, was perfumed with sensible sensors to orderly feel the material universe, which was created especially for him. Thus, the body became a channel for the joy of the material and spiritual delights of Creation, among which there were: the sunlight and the colours that pleased the eyes, the delicate and majestic sounds that pleased the ears, the wind, the warmth and the texture of the materials found in the Garden of Heaven, which pleased the tactile sensors, the skin, the hair, the teeth, etc., and other sensors of various kinds and suited for various needs.

The man, feeling bodily joy due to the somatic sensors, diverse feelings through his soul and God's love and order through his spirit, lived in happiness, his natural state of being, in Eden.

The Lord, making man in charge of a part of Creation by asking him to name the animals and knowing that it was high responsibility which required man to be tightly connected to the part of Creation he was in charge of, gave man a helper and an equal suited to his needs: the woman.

*"The man gave names to all livestock and to the birds of the heavens and to every beast of the field. **But for Adam there was not found a helper fit for him**. So the LORD God caused a deep sleep to fall upon the man, and while he slept took one of his ribs and closed up its place with flesh. The man said, "This is now bone of my bones and flesh of my flesh; she shall be called 'woman,' for she was taken out of man."* Genesis 2, 20-23

God blesses man by giving him a being even gentler than him, to help him materially and mostly spiritually. Man learns from woman and woman learns from man, continuously, God's love for them both, through the relationship that joins the two of them together.

Thus, man and woman start on the road of learning wisdom, a road laid before them by God, out of love for them:

"*And God blessed them. And God said to them, 'Be fruitful and multiply and fill the earth and subdue it and have dominion over the fish of the sea and over the birds of the heavens and over every living thing that moves on the earth'.*"

Soon, their wisdom was tested by means of a snake and a falsely good impulse which manipulated and took advantage of the naiveté and curiosity of the most delicate half of the couple, the women.

"*The snake said to the woman, 'Did God actually say, You shall not eat of any tree in the garden?'*"

And the woman said to the serpent, 'We may eat of the fruit of the trees in the garden, but God said, 'You shall not eat of the fruit of the tree that is in the midst of the garden, neither shall you touch it, lest you die."

*But the serpent said to the woman, '**You will not surely die**. For God knows that when you eat of it **your eyes will be opened, and you will be like God**, knowing good and evil.'"*

This incentive of Satan is craftily handled when given to man, as it is an incentive to improve the human condition, advice which God Himself had given to man in a different form when He had told him to master, to use the gifts properly. This shows that in the Garden of Heaven there was no fear, terror or pain, tools which the devil would use so many times throughout man's history after the Fall of Man, in order to make man obey him instead of the Lord. Thus, man thought the enticement to be good and, being brave by the nature given him by the Lord, his bravery came from his knowing he was free, untied by sins, he made an unwise decision, based on pride and not filtered through his obedience to the Lord. He wished to evolve fast and independently from the Lord's will and took the advice:

"So when the woman **saw that the tree was good for food**, and that it was a delight to the eyes, and that the tree was to be **desired to make one wise**, she took of its fruit and ate, and she also gave some to her husband who was with her, and he ate."

Right after tasting the divine fruit, man felt he had betrayed the principle of obedience because, although there were many things that he understood by the rapid accumulation of knowledge, he could not grasp the spiritual meaning of these things. More in depth, he did not understand the state of things as they were organized in God's plan, so he did not and still does not understand the world that he is living in.

Thus, man became estranged of his body and, oblivious of its sanctity and pure beauty, wanted to cover it to diminish their shame, the things they did not know or understand about their bodies or parts of them.

By eating from the fruit, man was able to see, but he did not see through the eyes of the Lord!

God adjusts His actions right away so that this creature may continue growing in wisdom and love. Through His actions, He shows that the plan for man's rehabilitation has already been completed and only needs to be followed step by step until man's healing and return to God's grace. God does not destroy Adam and Eve after they have broken His specific order, but asks where they are, why they are hiding and, seeing what has happened, curses the snake, shows first Eve, then Adam the consequences of their deed and then starts once again taking great care of them:

When Eve and Adam ate the fruit, their eyes became open and they saw their naked bodies. So they made clothes from leaves and covered themselves. After scolding them, God Himself makes better clothes for them, made from of animal hides.

And, to keep this error from becoming eternal, God expels Adam and Eve from the Garden of Eden and places Cherubims with flaming swords, so He introduces fear as a learning tool, showing His power in an accurate form, in order to close access to the Tree of Life, which had become dangerous for Adam's decayed condition.

For the first time, God reveals to Adam what will happen to his body.

"Because you have listened to the voice of your wife and have eaten of the tree of which I commanded you, 'You shall not eat of it,' cursed is the ground because of you; in pain you shall eat of it all the days of your life; thorns and thistles it shall bring forth for you;

And you shall eat the plants of the field.

By the sweat of your face you shall eat bread, till you return to the ground, for out of it you were taken; for you are dust, and to dust you shall return."

So this is how corporal death appears, no so much as punishment for man's mistake before God, but more as a key part of God's plan of restoring man to his initial glory. If death did not exist, then man's mistake would become eternal and there would be no turning back to his Father's arms, since we already know that although Satan did not die at all, he still does not want to recant his rebellion.

The first human victim of Death was Abel.

Cain's younger brother, Abel was a God-loving being. The Holy Scriptures say he was a shepherd who sacrificed to God the gentlest creatures in his care, so the best he had to offer:

"In the course of time Cain brought to the LORD an offering of the fruit of the ground, and Abel also brought of the firstborn of his flock and of their fat portions. And the LORD had regard for Abel and his offering".

God looked upon Abel with great joy and love. Cain, too, was looked upon with the same love, but not with joy, because Cain's gifts to the Lord spoke about the conflicts in the heart of Adam's first son. God encouraged Cain and showed him the path to wisdom, but he willingly chose the path laid before his parents by Satan, the path of disobedience.

Thus, Cain killed Abel, who was called an **innocent and righteous man** by the Saviour Himself and **a highly faithful** man by the words of the Holy Spirit:

*"So that on you may come all the righteous blood shed on earth, from the blood of **righteous Abel** to the blood of Zechariah the son of Barachiah, whom you murdered between the sanctuary and the altar"* Matthew 23, 35

"By faith Abel offered to God a more acceptable sacrifice than Cain, through which he was commended as righteous, God commending him by accepting his gifts. And through his faith, though he died, he still speaks." Hebrews 11:4

The righteous Abel entered, by death, a world where he waited in peace, not tormented like the non-believers, like those tied to Satan, until God reached Sheol, during the three days before His resurrection, and freed Abel from the slavery of Death, along with the other righteous men and patriarchs; and they were taken to Heaven, for the eternal life, to constantly look at the face of the Lord , which is plenitude of the life in God.

The sinful and unfaithful men who had not been righteous in their lives before the Flood and whom the Patriarchs after the Flood and the Prophets had not managed to bring back to faith remained in Hell, to wait for the Judgment Day, which will be the final event of God's Plan, the end of this parenthesis (the Life and Death of Man) which is part of the divine plan for man's redemption.

Man was not judged for his disobedience immediately after his fall and, so, he was given time to prepare for the final judgment throughout all of his life and death. With preparation, man can gain back God's grace and feel His mercy, which will save him from the temporary punishment of the first death, the death of the body:

"Shall I ransom them from the power of Sheol? Shall I redeem them from Death?" Hosea 13, 14

By the coming of Jesus Christ in the world, something fundamental changed in how Death operates as a step towards human redemption.

Jesus brings the news that man no longer needs to go to Hell for justice to be done and man to be redeemed, but that, immediately after the dormition of the body, the believer's spirit may be elevated now to Heaven, where the patriarchs, prophets and righteous men of all times now rest. This redemption from the punishment of death is possible only by mercy of the Lord, who does not wish to punish man more than necessary. Man could not enter heaven without being cleaned of his original sin, his disobedience in the Garden of Eden, and, by the Saviour's sacrifice on the cross, justice was done and the sin was punished. The disobedience was turned into obedience, as Jesus sacrificed Himself for us out of obedience to the Father and all those who lived as faultlessly as possible according to God's teachings were freed from the seal of death and could join the Lord their God at once.

There is an essential moment in the divine plan, which happens on the cross. As it was already shown before, God chased man away from the Garden of Eden and placed Cherubims with flaming swords to keep man from entering back. For thousands of years, man did not enter Heaven, he did not even see it from afar.

When the Saviour was on the cross and one of the thieves comforted Him and spoke in His defence, although he himself was in great pain, the Lord on the cross turned His face to the thief and spoke the sweetest words Adam wished to hear all his life after the Fall: *"Truly, I say to you, today you will be with me in Paradise"* Luke 23, 43

The forgiveness for the sin of disobedience, the forgiveness long awaited by Adam came directly from God's mouth and was heard by a man's ears.

Saint Silouan the Athonite speaks of Adam's sorrow, which stayed with him all his life:

"Adam, father of all mankind, in paradise knew the sweetness of the love of God; and so when for his sin he was driven forth from the garden of Eden and was widowed of the love of God, he suffered grievously and lamented with a mighty moan. And the whole desert rang with his lamentations. His soul was racked as he thought: 'I have grieved my beloved Lord". He sorrowed less after paradise and the beauty thereof – he sorrowed that he was bereft of the love of God, which insatiably, at every instant, draws the soul to Him." Saint Silouan the Athonite

Oh, how great were the joy and shock of that thief when he heard the words that had not been heard by anyone since the fall from the Garden of Eden! The thief's joy was even greater as, although a law-breaker and a poor man both materially and in virtues, he received the gift of being the first man to whom heaven was re-opened.

After the Saviour's rise to heaven, the apostles were empowered to absolve people after death and, so, the Church, that was built "Ad Litteram" with their hands, starts praying for those who, for one reason or another, went to hell to fulfil God's justice, in order to save them from eternal death. This spiritual work happened when the apostles gave to the priests the Holy Spirit by placing their hands on their head and to the people they gave the Holy Sacraments, among which Christ's body and blood, without which there is no eternal life.

The church helps the believer, baptised with the Holy Spirit while alive, to escape hell sooner in order to fulfil the Lord's mercy, which overflows as soon as and, sometimes, at the same time as justice is done: like the believers who, on their death bed, their death being the enforcement of the Lord's Justice, receive the holy sacraments, Baptism, the Holy Communion, and thus go straight to heaven, thus fulfilling also God's Mercy by a single act of passage from the earthly life to the heavenly one.

Death is both a punishment and mercy from God and, along with His other gifts and mercies, help man rise from the condition of creature demonised by disobedience and, later on, by the lack of faith, to a creature that is in harmony with the divine will and fully restored in the eyes of the beloved Creator.

In contrast with the fact that man has access to redemption through the judgement (the punishment) of death is the Devil, who remains forever separated from his Creator and who will not benefit from this spiritual tool, death, to get closer to God, because the difference between the Devil and man is, however incredible this seems to us, humans, that the Devil **does not wish** to get closer to the Creator and does not love Him, being seized by a perpetual, horrible, impossible, and thus frustrating wish of destroying God.

The physical death, especially after the coming of the Savior, brings joy to the soul of the believer as it is maybe the utmost material proof that life on this earth, which is still under the divine punishment, is given to us only so that we may know God again and learn and obey His rules, through which we will receive the Grace that will eventually set us free, even from this mercy of God, the Death.

Thus, the joy of the righteous is full at the time of their physical death, the divine justice and mercy being combined in this unique, key moment for which any man must prepare during his lifetime through faith and good deeds. Man must work his spirit so that, at the end of his life, death be a **return of the beloved Eden** and not **a second fall** caused by his lack of faith until the time of his death.

The first fall was human; the second fall is devilish.

The Road to the Ladder of Infinite Glory

The life of man, even his destiny are seen in the light of his fall from the divine grace back when he lived with his beloved and merciful God in the Garden of Eden.

But, while most eyes, however well or ill advised, turn to repairing this regrettable fact, piercing this evil sphere we have been living in since the Fall and until present, it would be recommendable to turn our eyes once in a while to the incredible future that God has and has always had in store for us, the future that awaits us once we reenter God's grace, after our death, after the waters of the Great Judgement and Great Repair, the redemption of Man, become still again.

When man is fully united with God and no trace of shame has remained in his soul or when he lives with the angels and in a way similar to them, with his dignity unstained, white as snow before his God, amazing things will happen, things that have been promised since the beginning, godly things that will reflect in each of us and will define each of us, who will manage to get there.

God put the Tree of Knowledge and the Tree of Life in the Garden of Eden so that man, under God's guidance and obedience, be able in time to eat from them both and thus become a chosen vessel of Creation, getting closer with each godly gift to an infinity of gifts and graces reserved for him personally since the beginning of Creation.

God promised and God shall keep His word: despite man's fall and the wish of his enemy, the accuser, man will be repaired. God had decided. Who can oppose God's decision? And God's decision is that Man will receive all the inheritance reserved for him.

Man has been made delicate and complex, so delicate that he seems weak, but his frail body hides a soul that can receive infinite gifts and energies and graces and all of these have been promised to him by the Supreme Being that does not lie and that is All-Powerful. Moreover, it has been decided that he would receive them in spite of man's first Fall or of the opposition of his enemy, the Accuser. No one can oppose God's decision of enriching man beyond any limit. And whoever believes that the Lord will not be able to keep His decision and promise does not know the Lord.

The nine hosts of angels known in the tradition of the church show us that the beings created by God with His energies are organised in a certain structure within Creation. Nevertheless, man does not have a fixed place and, although he is now inferior to the heavenly hosts in God's plan, there have been cases of people, e.g. the Virgin Mary, St. Paul the Apostle taken from the Third Heaven, which show us that man's place in the structure of Creation is free and even meant for self-improvement:

"Do you not know that we will judge angels?"
1 Corinthians 6, 3

How else can one explain the opening of the skies to receive a man, Jesus Christ and, through Him, another human being, the Virgin Mary, and yet another, Saint Paul, the Apostle received directly in the Third Heaven, if not by God's declared purpose of glorifying man above all others?

The Apostle Paul says:
"Are not all angels ministering spirits sent to serve those who will inherit salvation?" Hebrews 1, 14

When God created man, He did not make him so that he should fall and then redeem himself, but that he obey the Lord from the very beginning and rise to the utmost glory and life in God. The Lord never meant for man to fall.

His purpose was to create a being before whom the entire body of angels would stand in awe, a being whom Jesus Christ celebrates and rises to the highest glory, by assuming the shape and being of this creature, according to the Holy Ecumenical Synods:

"We, then, following the holy Fathers, all with one consent, teach men to confess one and the same Son, our Lord Jesus Christ, the same perfect in Godhead and also perfect in manhood; truly God and truly man, of a reasonable [rational] soul and body; consubstantial [co-essential] with the Father according to the Godhead, and consubstantial with us according to the Manhood; in all things like unto us, without sin; begotten before all ages of the Father according to the Godhead, and in these latter days, for us and for our salvation, born of the Virgin Mary, the Mother of God, according to the Manhood; one and the same Christ, Son, Lord, only begotten, to be acknowledged in two natures, inconfusedly, unchangeably, indivisibly, inseparably; the distinction of natures being by no means taken away by the union, but rather the

property of each nature being preserved, and concurring in one Person and one Subsistence, not parted or divided into two persons, but one and the same Son, and only begotten, God the Word, the Lord Jesus Christ; as the prophets from the beginning [have declared] concerning Him, and the Lord Jesus Christ Himself has taught us, and the Creed of the holy Fathers has handed down to us." THE FOURTH COUNCIL OF CHALCEDON

The grace of God that lies within the Lord Jesus Christ overflows, through the sacrament of His union with man, in the Virgin Mary, the Mother of God, who is rightfully praised in church:

"More honorable than the cherubim, and beyond compare more glorious than the seraphim" Axion Estin

As promised by God, man breaks through the barriers of the structure of Creation, which organises the hosts of angels and the skies full of grace, and is given access to the road of grandeur, glory, spiritual growth and continuous evolution, free, without obstacles, ceaselessly unblocking new spiritual perspectives so as to look back and appreciate his road started... today.

At some point in the New Testament, the Lord Jesus Christ scolds the people for their lack of faith in God's promises, saying:

"Who of you by worrying can add a single hour to his life?

"And why do you worry about clothes? See how the lilies of the field grow. They do not labor or spin. Yet I tell you that not even Solomon in all his splendor was dressed like one of these. If that is how God clothes the grass of the field, which is here today and tomorrow is thrown into the fire, will he not much more clothe you, O you of little faith? So do not worry, saying, 'What shall we eat?' or 'What shall we drink?' or 'What shall we wear?' For the pagans run after all these things, and your heavenly Father knows that you need them. But seek first his kingdom and his righteousness, and all these things will be given to you as well. Therefore do not worry about tomorrow, for tomorrow will worry about itself. Each day has enough trouble of its own." Matthew 6, 27-34

In his wish to reach the glory and gifts promised by the Lord, man needs only to stay still and silently rejoice, to work slowly, but surely for his own and others' redemption, to continuously obey the Lord, certain that, once this redemption is completed, the

Lord will clothe him with all the glory and gifts unheard of which are his inheritance.

And with little effort from man and lots of faith in the Lord and His promises, the day will come when the skies will open and the voice of the Almighty Lord will thunder from up in the sky:

"Quick! Bring the best robe and put it on him. Put a ring on his finger and sandals on his feet. Bring the fattened calf and kill it. Let's have a feast and celebrate."
Parable of the Prodigal Son – Luke 15, 22-23

So help us God. Amen.

‘

THE END

Post Scriptum

Points of Perspective

Back in the time of the Kingdom of David, common people thought that they lived poorly and that the good times of Abraham were gone, times when access to the land was open and free, they could peacefully and safely admire the wealth of life, there was plenty of land with no fences, for everyone to share, and the animals were left to graze wherever they pleased.

In the time of the Roman Empire, the people of Israel spoke only words of praise about the Kingdom of David and lamented about the Roman oppression, especially about the fact that they had to be counted down to the last man (the census) for tax purposes, that the taxes were high and they could not speak freely without fear of being found and destroyed along with their families. But the honorable citizens, the peasants and farmers and the people in the cities had their land measured in square miles, and the animals had preset grazing lands.

Nowadays, we find that the time of the Roman Empire was beautiful because of all the freedom there was for certain major groups of people: the freedom to hold enough land, to not go each day to the same routinous work, to not have a scheduled life after the 9-to-5 corporate work, plus traffic time. Nowadays, we are trapped in the modern slavery, ultra-counted for dozens and hundreds of taxes and checked a thousand times lest we should step out of formation. Nowadays, we measure the land we own by a few dozens of square feet and we no longer keep animals. Even if we did, we wouldn't have the means to raise them. Few exceptions.

Little by little, there will come a time when our children's children will talk about the happy days of the present, when they could still see a tree in a small 10 by 10 meters yard, or a few tomatoes or flowers grown in the back yard. Maybe at that point, they will complain about their modern times, full only of insignificant, meaningless work, lack of priority and of time, about the lack of time to actually enjoy life. With exceptions in a few places long forgotten. A few or none at all.

Maybe a man in the Kingdom of David, while lying on his back in a field of flowers, munching a blade of grass, had he been able to see into the future, would have enjoyed more the "little" he had, which nowadays he would consider as fabulous wealth: food from his fields, gardens, vineyards, orchards and animals, many relatives in the kitchen, talking and laughing while preparing tasty meals for the entire family; the feeling of safety given by the friendly looks of the relatives, neighbors and friends in the familiar places; the free time left by the work seasons, the wealth of the land, the light of day and the darkness of the night.

Time to ponder on the wealth of life on earth…
Time to ponder on the wealth of the life after the life on earth…
In order to replant hope and the joy of life from where they have disappeared, from the future of mankind, here are a few words of God's eternal message to men, words that float on the wings of God's power to hand us the magnificent gift of hope:

> "Every man will sit under his own vine and under his own fig tree, and no one will make them afraid, for the Lord Almighty has spoken." Micah 4, 4

> "And I heard a loud voice from the throne saying, "Now the dwelling of God is with men, and he will live with them. They will be his people, and God himself will be with them and be their God. He will wipe every tear from their eyes. There will be no more death or mourning or crying or pain, **for the old order of things has passed away.**" Revelation 21, 3-5

Front Cover Illustration:

"Jacob Wrestling with the Angel"
by Alexander Louis Leloi

Book Cover Design: Catalin Damir

First Edition 2013

ISBN-13: 978-0992063504

ISBN-10: 0992063507

www.ingramcontent.com/pod-product-compliance
Lightning Source LLC
Chambersburg PA
CBHW051749040426
42446CB00007B/286